When A Family Reaches For The American Dream

When Jon Masters was 10, his parents, seeking access to the American upper class, cut off their families, became Episcopalians, and made him promise not to tell anyone they had ever been Jews – not any woman he might marry, and not his brother who was in the crib in the next room. For more than 30 years, he lived parallel lives: in one he was constrained by his parents' fears of exposure; in the other he acted as if his family's past did not exist and he could be whoever he wanted to be.

Within the family his father was in charge, threatening to die if the secret was revealed. In his public life, Jon believed he was immune to the consequences of denial. He went to top schools, was mentored by high ranking superiors, and as a young naval officer was marked for success among a circle of seasoned Washington policy-makers.

By the time he was 40, it all started to come apart. He didn't know who he was. By then, he was a father and a husband. He had no confidantes and held his wife at arm's length for fear of exposing the secret and terrified of the consequences of doing so.

This is the story of what brought him to that point and what he did to protect his children, save his marriage, maintain his career, and nourish his soul. Family took precedence over power and healing the family trauma became his priority. Helping his children become independent, caring, and accomplished in ways of their own choosing was his goal.

JON J. MASTERS

FEAR, FATHERS and FAMILY

In Search of the American Dream

outskirtspress
DENVER, COLORADO

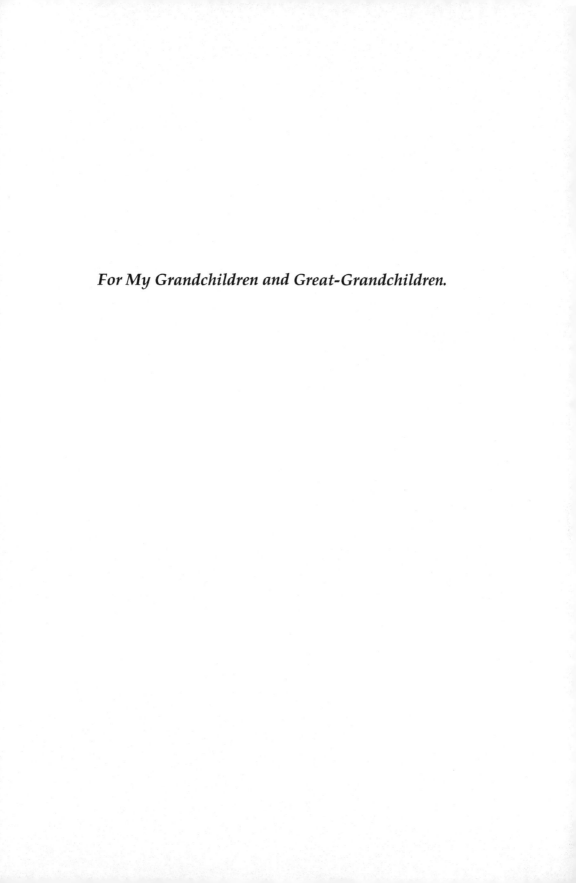

For My Grandchildren and Great-Grandchildren.

Table of Contents

Preface

I know very little about my grandparents and almost nothing about my great-grandparents. They were not part of my life and my parents would not tell me about them. My parents felt the past was not relevant. I disagree. It influences the present. We can learn from the past, and I want my grandchildren and great-grandchildren to have that opportunity.

What follows is the story of how I found my way in life – the joys, the sorrows. The issues I had. The challenges I faced. The ways I coped. The mistakes I made. The successes I enjoyed. The lessons I learned. The person I became.

It is my life as I remember it. The stories are a reflection of who I think I am, and that is complicated. I write from my perspective. Others may see things differently. Objectivity may not be possible. Truth is also elusive as memory.

My life is more than what I did. What I did can be researched. How I felt about it cannot, and that is what these stories are about. They are not a resume of my accomplishments. They reflect what is significant to me about my life, which may or may not be important to others. They are also written with a view to what would be interesting to my grandchildren and great-grandchildren, so that good times with friends whom they would not know did not make the cut.

My hope is that by sharing my life stories I will have opened for my descendants a window on their past which will enrich their lives. And I hope that other readers will find life lessons as well.

Introduction

For more than 30 years, I lived parallel lives: one tightly constrained by the family secret, living in fear of exposure like a trembling social outcast. In the other, I was in revolt against the secret but too afraid to reveal it; my past did not exist – I was ambitious, smart and could be whoever I wanted to be.

In the first case, my father was in charge of my life, but not entirely of his own. He had bet his life on my maintaining the secret "for my own good." If I revealed it, he threatened at my bedside, he would die, and I believed him.

In my second life, I was in charge and believed myself to be immune to the consequences of denial. While my parents focused on appearances not substance, I went to first-rate schools, was mentored by prominent high achievers, and as a young naval officer was marked for success among a circle of seasoned Washington policy-makers. As a mere apprentice with a voice in politico-military affairs, I was arrogant enough to envision becoming Secretary of State.

By the time I was 40, it all started to come apart. I lost my way. I didn't know who I was – a rising star or an outcast? By then, I was a father and a husband myself. Where did those roles coalesce? What price was I willing to pay to feed my ambitions? I had no confidante. I held my wife at arm's length for fear of exposing the secret and terrified of the consequences of doing so. It was a double bind. By refusing to open up, I was pushing her away. My marriage was at stake.

This is the story of what brought me to that point and what I did to protect my children, save my marriage, maintain my career, and nourish my soul. I broke. I told my wife – and my brother – the secret. My father died a year later at the age of 74.

I had to pick up the pieces and build a new life. My priorities had changed, and success looked different. Neither acceptance nor achievement was sufficient. Family took precedence over power and healing the family trauma became my priority. Helping my children become independent, caring, and accomplished in ways of their own choosing was my goal. How to do that, given my past, and still have a successful career was my challenge. Here's what I went through and how I found my way.

I.

My Family

I was born on Fathers' Day, 1937, to a father who looked like John Barrymore and a mother as beautiful as any movie star. They were chic, they were glamorous, and they were on the rise. They had just rented a Park Avenue penthouse with a surrounding terrace. My father's law practice was growing: he represented band leaders, song writers, hotel owners, and young men in line to run successful family businesses. They were all Jews, and so were we.

My mother's father built one and two-family homes in Brooklyn where he and my grandmother lived. My father's father – he died before I was born – had been, according to the local newspaper, "one of the best known Jewish residents of Greater Pittston," Pennsylvania. If there was discrimination against Jews, it did not seem to affect us. We had Jewish friends and relatives whom we visited from time to time. My father was one of 11 children, and my mother was one of 6. We were prospering.

I didn't know what simmered beneath that surface – the tensions and history that would come to dominate my life. My mother's paternal grandparents had owned a factory in or near

Odessa which made either the wheels for the czar's coaches or the coaches themselves. The Cossacks came one night in 1905, destroyed the factory, murdered my great-grandfather and probably other family members, looted and burnt their houses. Next year my mother's parents left for the United States. They survived, but the pogrom had traumatized them and they were unable to give my mother much, if any, emotional support. She talked to me about being lonely as a child. "I played endlessly with my doll, but I was always well dressed and well cared for," she said – a pattern she repeated with me.

Although her parents lived only a subway ride away, I don't think I saw them more than half a dozen times – and always at their house in a lower middle class neighborhood in Brooklyn. I saw my maternal grandfather only once, and don't remember ever seeing my mother's brothers and sisters. I didn't even know most of their names until recently when my wife Rosemary's sister-in-law discovered them while researching my mother's family genealogy (my grandfather's name was Louis and my grandmother's was Bessie.) As far as I can recall, no one from my mother's family ever came to our apartment, and I never saw my father with any of them. My father never went with us when we visited my mother's family. A cousin claimed that my mother's family was angry at my father because he failed to get an acquittal for one of my mother's brothers who was charged during Prohibition with some offense involving large amounts of liquor found in the family garage. As a result, my mother's brother could not become a lawyer, and, according to his son, this ruined his life. It is also possible that my father never showed up because he wanted nothing to do with my mother's family, and my mother never pressed him on it.

I never viewed my mother's family as my family. I knew

*My parents A. Edward and Shady Masters
around the time of my birth, 1937*

nothing about them except that they lived in a white clapboard house with a front porch and a kitchen in the rear where my grandmother fed me, gave me toys to play with, and left me while she and my mother visited in the next room. The same emotional distance that had so affected my mother's childhood was evident in my grandmother's relationship with me. If she now talked with my mother, she made little attempt to communicate with me. Looking back, I realize that neither my mother nor my grandmother had ever given me an opportunity to learn about the family. As I have grown older, I regret never hearing any stories about life in Russia. It is quite likely, however, that given the trauma of the pogrom, my grandmother was reluctant to speak about her past. As it was, my mother's family figured in my life only through the effect they had on my mother.

The family I knew was my father's. They were real people to me – even though my grandfather had died before I was born. Joseph Moskowitz came to the United States in 1887 at the age of 17 from Zeplene, then in Austro-Hungary, now Slovakia. Like many Eastern European Jews, he lived on Manhattan's lower Eastside – 130 Goerck Street – and made his living selling I don't know what – household items, clothes? – from a push-cart. But after a year or so of scraping by, at his brother-in-law's urging, he moved to Pittston, Pennsylvania where opportunities were said to be greater. The 1900 census lists Joseph's occupation as a grocer; he was running the general store – the family lived upstairs – in Port Griffith, a speck of a town on the ridge between Scranton and Wilkes-Barre. The 1910 census lists him as a merchant and the 1920 census as a merchant and a grocer – "the well-known Port Griffith merchant," according to the local paper. Joseph was a good businessman, and the general store was a success. I have no doubt that the help of his numerous children kept costs down. In addition to running the store, he made a lot of money in third mortgages. A pious Orthodox Jew, he also financed the first temple constructed in the area.

According to my father, my grandfather "was a tyrant. He gave orders and we had to obey." My father hated to answer to his father – or anyone. Ironically, and probably inevitably, he modeled his adult behavior on his father's and tried to control me and everyone else around him with an iron hand. He also spoke bitterly of the abuse he took as a Jew. "When I walked to school, neighborhood kids threw rocks at me and called me Jew-boy."

As long as his mother was alive we visited his family in Pennsylvania. We traveled first class – the Pullman car – on the trains that took us for weekends to Scranton, where most of the family lived. Chauffeured Carey Cadillacs carried us to Long Island for occasional Sunday meals with his oldest sister's family. Was my father showing off?

My grandmother Rose, a five-foot dynamo who had given birth to 11 children and still remained slim and attractive, was always warm and welcoming when we visited. There was food or candy in every room, and like most Jewish grandmothers, she was not happy unless the family finished off the huge platters on the table. "Eat up," she would say – as if I wasn't already a bit overweight. Rose might have been small, but she was in charge. Her "requests" were orders. None of my aunts, uncles or cousins ever argued with her or ignored her bidding. Even my father obeyed. He did not seem to resent her demands as he hated those of his father. Had she tried to protect him from his father's tyranny? Who knows? But they shared a warmth that did not exist with others in the family. My father once told me, "I couldn't leave the family or change my religion while my mother was alive." When she died, he did just that.

My father had little love for his male siblings. He was "the golden boy", the smartest, the best-looking, and the most accomplished – destined for success, and he saw his family as a hindrance to his ambition. Everyone had a say in decisions – which interfered with his own desire for independence. He described his brothers in terms I had difficulty relating to because they were not the way I perceived them. Perhaps he was trying to justify his abandoning his family. He said his oldest brother, Doc, was a third rate dentist who ruined the teeth of everyone in the family and who "steered me to a second rate school – Syracuse – when I could have gone to a much better one." In fact, my father claimed to have transferred from Syracuse to Penn after two or three years. While I could never confirm this, I remember him taking me to a couple of Penn-Cornell football games as if he were a returning alumnus. He described his brother Max as an alcoholic card shark, and saw Sam as an incompetent lawyer whom he fired from his law firm. Walter was a polo-playing ne'er-do-well who always needed money. Of his five sisters, only Anna, the eldest, seemed to hold his affection for she was the only one we would visit.

His characterizations were hardly fair, but they influenced my view of the family. As much as I wanted uncles and aunts and cousins, I grew apart from them. It was as though they were on the inside, and I was on the outside. They may not have been as smart or as high-powered as my father – though I question that now as I look at how successful some of them were. And whatever their faults, when I was a small child, they embraced me. Doc played chess with me. Sam brought me presents. Walter and I had pillow fights.

My father saw only their failures and belittled their accomplishments. When Sam left the law, he became a successful stockbroker. Walter landed at Normandy on D-Day and was appointed mayor of one of the first French towns the allies captured. Later he became a consul in the American diplomatic corps and served in Turin, Italy and Dakar, Senegal. If he didn't shine at his jobs, he did enjoy the women and the parties – and later did reasonably well in advertising. My father's sisters – with the exception of Ida whose poodle-cloth coats somehow remain in my mind as a mark of her character and who was eventually institutionalized – were intelligent women who raised talented offspring.

Anna's two sons and a daughter, my first cousins, were much older than me and I did not realize how talented they were: Bobby was a naval officer who later became a partner in an accounting firm. I remember at age 5 feeling proud to sit next to him while he drove us to New York from Scranton in his navy blue officer's uniform; Marvin was a Navy enlisted man who took over his father-in-law's uniform business; and Joan was in college on the way to becoming a stalwart volunteer in her Long Island community. Ella had two children: Sheldon a doctor at Columbia Presbyterian; and Allan a student at Amherst who later became a highly respected lawyer and senior partner of the largest law firm in the Wilkes-Barre area

What I did know was my father's demeaning attitude towards the family: they were not going to amount to much. I was a confident New York kid ready to do battle with whomever or whatever challenged me. If that was my family, I blush now to admit that I sided with my father-- get me out of there! My father was wrong, of course, but as a kid I didn't realize that.

Both my parents were certain that they were better than

their relatives and believed they were entitled to the best the world had to offer. Jewish or not, they were going to get it. Like James Gatz who reinvented himself as Jay Gatsby in F. Scott Fitzgerald's *The Great Gatsby*, my parents believed, like millions of other immigrants' children, that renaming themselves was the first step to achieving the American dream. Growing up in the 1920s, they were captivated by elegance and style – they wanted to join the lavish parties where men in white ties and tails embraced beautiful women in ball gowns. The glamorous life called for dancing the Charleston in speakeasies and drinking bootleg gin and champagne. My mother recalled, "It was a time of fun and freedom. We could be whoever we wanted to be."

Appearances were crucial. It did not matter that Jay Gatsby never opened any books in his library; their presence was enough to establish his credentials. My parents understood this. How things looked was what counted. They judged people by how they dressed, and immediately wrote off those who did not live up to their standards. My father enhanced his own image by spending lavishly where his largesse could be noticed, by the wines he served, the people he befriended, and the activities he enjoyed like owning race horses and joining the Turf and Field Club, whose members – society's first families – became nodding acquaintances.

My mother, a queen of style, bought all my father's clothes and furnished the beautiful spacious new apartment in which I grew up from the age of 3. It was in one of the finest Art Deco buildings in New York – unusually classy for a building that accepted Jews. Friends and visitors admired the apartment, especially the way my mother had decorated it with elegant looking "antiques" and gorgeous fabrics. The antiques were just copies,

purchased at a discount by my mother who had somehow gotten an interior decorator's license for this purpose alone. As
far as I know, she never worked in that business although she
would probably have been very successful had she tried. The
large living room, about 20 x 20, was dominated in one corner
by a grand piano that was usually out of tune and rarely played
once I stopped taking piano lessons. Two love seats – uphol-
stered in green and white so they would always look fresh –
faced each other on either side of the fireplace where a fire was
prepared but never lit. Directly across from the fireplace on the
opposite wall a long coffee table stood in front of an enormous
but comfortable sofa. Tables and chairs were scattered before
the paintings and bookcases that lined the walls. But the im-
pressive appearance was deceiving. The only original furniture
or art in the room – other than small paintings of my brother
and me – were an English 18th century pie-crust table and an
18th century piano chair. Everything else was a copy. I am pretty
certain we could have afforded real antiques but reproductions
were cheaper and my mother didn't care. The look, not the substance, was what counted.

I was very much part of my parents' plans. As their foot
soldier on the front lines I was expected to breach the social
barriers for them. They hoped to piggyback on whatever success I might have with the parents of my school friends. As a
child of privilege they gave me opportunities they never had:
a Park Avenue apartment, governesses, nice clothes, private
schools, society dance classes, and Social Register friends who
welcomed me to their homes and included me in their activities. Years later, my father told me, "I wanted to be you." Doors
opened for me that, despite all their attempts, remained more
or less closed to them. By the time I was 10 and burdened with

the family secret, I realized that my parents' demand that I excel at every activity arose from their fear that I might slip up, and explode their chance to realize their dreams.

With so much going for me, how could I complain when things went against me? I certainly couldn't complain to them. And I didn't. I was a cheerful, determined kid who, as my mother often said, "would always whistle in the dark." I liked being out front. I was going to give my parents a shot at the American dream. In the process I actually achieved it for myself. I certainly learned how to be brash.

II.

My First Ten Years

I spent my first six months in a Park Avenue penthouse apartment – judging by family pictures, mostly on the terrace with few or no clothes on. My parents, probably my mother, worried about my health, would not allow anyone to take me downstairs, much less to the street or Central Park until I was six months old. From the family photos, it looks like they would also not allow anyone to cut my hair for six months – typical for the time.

I think my mother thought of me as her doll. She kept me in a dress until I was six months old and thereafter in what she thought most fashionable. She had an eye for style, not practicality. In warmer weather, I was dressed in white, except for a red and white-striped linen jacket. In cooler weather, it was grey flannels, a fitted navy blue coat with brass buttons and a red lining, and a felt hat with a feather. Whatever the weather, I wore white gloves. When I got to the park, the governess put overalls over my fancy clothes. Before I left the park, the overalls came off to restore my elegant appearance for the trip home. How I looked was very important to my mother. In dressing me, she was not only oblivious to the realities of how children play, she was also oblivious to what was going on in the world. In 1940 or 1941, when Austrians and Germans were terrorizing Jews, she proudly dressed me in a green and gray Tyrolean outfit.

My mother had a great eye for color and design, and she boasted, "I never paid retail." When she was young, she would spot a dress in a store, take it home on trial, give it to her dressmaker to copy, and then return the original to the store. Some of the saleswomen caught on, but never stopped her. At her death, her clothes, beautiful and fashionable, (20 racks!) were gratefully accepted by a non-profit thrift shop.

Did she love me? I never knew. One experience in particular still puzzles me. One night when I was about 7 or 8, my mother came to my room to say goodnight before leaving with my father for an evening of dinner and dancing. She looked terrific. "You look so pretty in that purple hat," I told her. She never wore that hat again.

What is it that makes that memory so vivid? I knew how important appearances and good clothes were to my mother. I wanted her to know I admired her. I wanted to bond with her. It didn't happen. Was it my fault or hers? I tried to hug her, but I had to settle for a goodnight kiss – one that would not disturb her make-up. Maybe she took offense that I had not complimented her on other occasions.

Spontaneous expression of emotions in parenting were beyond my mother's capability and quite likely, beyond her comprehension: given a childhood in which her own parents had ignored her. This doesn't mean we did not have some good times together. It just meant we didn't talk about our feelings. Actually, we rarely talked about anything of substance.

I'm uncertain about my mother's love, but I'm sure she cared about me, as well as she could. When I was in grammar

Me in a Tyrolean outfit about 1941

school, she faithfully attended all my school plays and soccer games. My father was too busy. At the end of every school term, she took me to lunch at Hamburger Heaven, and on Thursday nights when my father was not home, she would go into the kitchen and make candy. It was the only thing she knew how to cook because my father – I think as a matter of pride – did not want his wife to work in the kitchen. Then she would take me to the movies. Those were good times.

Shopping for clothes with my mother was not much fun. She always looked for the best fit at the lowest price. The stores that sold boys' clothes were all within a few blocks of each other on Madison and Fifth Avenues. I would try on a blazer I liked in one shop, where the price was comparable to what we had paid the previous year. My mother usually told the salesman, "Please hold it for us." Then she would take me to three or four other stores to see if she could find a better price or a better blazer. All the blazers looked the same to me and differed little in price. My lifelong aversion to wandering through shops looking for interesting or original clothes is rooted in these shopping trips with my mother. Nonetheless, she left a mark: even today, clothes are important to me, and I pride myself on being well turned out. Maybe dressing well is part of my armor against the feeling that I am an interloper and don't belong.

My mother's efforts at intellectual stimulation started and ended when she hired a Swiss nanny to teach me French. When (according to my mother) I told the nanny to "Stop speaking funny," the nanny was fired and replaced by Harriet. Thank God.

From the time I was three until I was five, Harriet Samuels was my main emotional support and my first love. I talked to her about my feelings; she listened and responded. She told me stories. She was warm. She cared. She encouraged me and bucked me up when I was down. I remember pleading with her, "Wait for me. I want to marry you." She read to me and taught me to read. Harriet had been a nursery school teacher before she took the job as my governess and she taught me a great deal; when I was five and a half, my first grade teacher said I already knew everything they were going to teach in first grade and I was moved into second grade.

Harriet left or was sent away while I was in summer camp. I think the latter. My mother did things like that whenever I was away: she gave away my dog, she rearranged my room. She never asked me what I wanted or how I felt about it. She just did what she wanted and I had to accept it. When I came back from camp and found Harriet gone, I was very upset, but I don't think I cried. I just went on to the next thing. Harriet wrote me to say she had gone to California and was getting married. I never saw her again, but in one way she never left me. My warmth – my ability to love – I owe to Harriet.

I don't remember my mother, or my father for that matter, ever taking me to a museum. I went to museums only on school outings or with friends. We did, however, go to the theater. I saw almost every Broadway hit: *South Pacific* with Mary Martin and Ezio Pinza, *Annie Get Your Gun* with Ethel Merman, *Mr. Roberts* with Henry Fonda, *Showboat, Pal Joey,* and on and on. Sometimes we would decide at dinner that we wanted to go to a show that evening, and my father would get tickets from a scalper. When we decided to go to the third performance of *South Pacific* after its rave reviews, my father was outraged at the price, "$16.49 a ticket for good orchestra seats!" my father bellowed into the phone. But he paid, and we went.

I was about six years old sitting on the jump seat of a large

yellow cab on our way to seeing *Life with Father* when I announced, "I'm going to be an actor." My parents didn't object. The theater was the single intellectual pursuit my parents
seemed to support. Maybe they felt safe in the theatre since most
Broadway musicals were written by Jews who had changed
their names – Irving Berlin, Lerner and Loewe, Rodgers and
Hart, Rodgers and Hammerstein, George and Ira Gershwin, *et
al*. They not only lived the American dream, they defined it. It
was Irving Berlin (born Israel Isidore Beilin) who wrote *White
Christmas, Easter Parade,* and *God Bless America.*

Although we went often to the theater, we never talked
about the plays. I don't know whether my mother couldn't, or
my father wouldn't. What I do know is that they were not very
interested in ideas. They did not read books and as a child neither did I. I associated reading with schoolwork, not pleasure.

I never had a substantive discussion with my parents on any
subject that did not relate directly to my conduct: no discussions of current events or public affairs or even sports. Learning
for learning's sake was an unknown concept to my father,
whose interests were truly utilitarian. He had no interest in ab-
stractions or even in politics – at least he never talked about
either; the test was whether something was currently useful.
Conversations with my mother were monologues about her social life and conversations with my father were lectures.

While my mother seemed to float on the surface of my life,
my father was invasive. He was deeply involved in my upbringing – perhaps too deeply, vacillating from being overly
nice to being terribly harsh – a pattern I saw him repeat in his
relations with others throughout his life. He often bought me
things that irritated my mother. I am told that one Christmas
my father decided that I did not have enough presents under

the tree, so on Christmas Eve he bought me half a dozen more. My mother was not happy.

On another occasion when I was 14, we were staying for a month at a hotel in Pine Orchard, Connecticut. I knew no one, and my only source of entertainment was the hotel's golf course. However, I needed golf clubs if I was going to play. The golf pro was selling clubs but they were more expensive than any in Manhattan. My father bought the golf clubs from the pro, and my mother went ballistic. "How could [I] always be in such a rush? What a waste of money!" When later in life I wanted something she didn't want to give me or didn't think I should have, she would declare, "It's just like the golf clubs."

I am not sure why my mother was so tight about money. Perhaps it was because she grew up poor. Maybe my father kept her on a short leash. Once she complained to me, "Your father hasn't raised my monthly allowance in 10 years." I wondered about this because in general my father was free with his money – as long as he decided how it would be spent. My father did not grow up in poverty. I had the sense my father rarely spent money for pleasure. Money had a purpose: he used it to curry favor, to show off: we always went first class (Pullman train or a chauffeured Carey Cadillac) whenever we visited his family, or to project an image.

While my father sometimes spoiled me with presents at other times he terrorized me. When I was about eight, I ripped my corduroy pants going over a wire fence on a farm in Dobbs Ferry on the Hudson River. I was on a school outing, and something impelled me to go over that fence. I looked up and saw a horse galloping in my direction. Scared, I ran to get back over the fence, ripping my pants in the process. When I got home, my mother raged at me, "That's the third pair of corduroys you have ripped. Your father will deal with you!" My father called me into his den. He was only five foot eight, but he seemed like a giant. Glaring, he proceeded to grill me on how I had ripped my pants. I knew better than to argue with him but I had to do something. Since I was not supposed to have gone over the fence in the first place, I told him, "I tripped playing ball." My father would have none of it. "You're lying," he said. "Don't you ever lie to me!" This was not an ordinary lecture. He ordered me to stand up straight and spoke daggers. He was a hanging judge declaring me guilty of a heinous crime and about to pass sentence. I was shaking. Had he physically threatened or beaten me, I might have been less traumatized. As I write this, I am not sure what made him so angry– especially about lying --when his own record of truth-telling was anything but resplendent.

I was expected to be tough. One Saturday my father took me skiing on Cedar Hill in Central Park. Skiing down the hill I crashed into a tree and ended up with one ski on either side of the tree, just like the *New Yorker* cartoon. I knew I was hurt and wanted to go home, but my father wouldn't let me. "Get up and ski," he commanded. I did – for about another hour; then we went home. The next morning when I tried to get out of bed, I could barely raise my torso and couldn't bend my legs. I slid out of bed and slithered into my parents' bedroom: "Dad, I think something is wrong." I had torn all the ligaments in my right knee and bruised my left. My knees played tricks on me for years afterward. Was I angry at him? Upset at what he had caused? I simply accepted him as he was. My father didn't listen. He had all the answers. It was certainly not the way I wanted to deal with my kids. On the other hand, I learned to get up and keep going – a valuable lesson for life.

One day, a few years later, I was walking home from school

with a classmate – three years older and a foot taller than I was. We were walking past a doorman building on Park Avenue and 88th Street when two boys about my size confronted us, "You got a dime? Give it to us." We tried to walk past them. My friend ran off but I stood my ground, refused to turn over the few cents I had in my pocket, was punched in the face and came home with a black eye. I don't know whether the doorman didn't see what was happening or chose to ignore it. I didn't expect help. My parents noted I had a black eye, but were not particularly interested in what had happened. Did my father tell me "it's not a big deal"? Whether he said it or not, I remember thinking, "OK, that's the way it is. I'm on my own." I was 11.

Despite everything, I looked up to my father. He worked very hard and often came home late. Like most people in those days, my father generally went to his office for half a day on Saturday. And sometimes he took me with him. As we rode the Lexington Avenue subway to his office, my father read his neatly folded newspaper. I admired the way he folded the newspaper so that it was compact, yet allowed him to easily find and read what he wanted. In those days it was primarily the stock tables; later on it was the horse racing charts.

My father's office was in a suite on a high floor at 80 Broad Street. His name, "A Edward Masters, Attorney" was prominently embossed on the glass portion of the door to the suite. His corner office opened onto a small terrace with a spectacular view of the ships entering the New York Harbor and the East River. He was "a big shot." His brother Sam worked for him as an associate lawyer as did Bert Field. Their office was in the file room on the other side of the suite. My father was as demanding at work as he was at home, so I was told, and given my own experience with him, I readily believed it. I think my father fired both of them. I never knew the facts, but firing his brother Sam couldn't have been pleasant. When I met Bert Field again many years later, he was still angry with my father.

When I came to the office, my father gave me a yellow pad and told me to visit with whomever was in the file room. I think I was just a bother to Sam and Bert. Because my father treated them like lackeys, I probably didn't treat them with much respect, and they weren't particularly welcoming. We ignored each other. At lunchtime my father and I would go to nearby restaurants for a swell meal. On one occasion, I got my father to go up to Nassau Street and, against what he thought was his better judgment, he bought me a Royal typewriter. "Why would you want to learn to type? Where would you ever use a typewriter?" he said. "It's a waste of money." He couldn't understand. But he bought the typewriter. I felt he would do anything for me then. I was ten.

Going with my father made me feel important, like I was a grown-up. I particularly remember a trip we made to Chicago when I was eight. During breakfast at the Parker House my father told me that the Brooklyn Dodgers were staying at the hotel, pointed to some of them in the dining room, and suggested, "Why don't you go over and talk to them while I go to my appointment." As soon as my father left, I walked over to the table where Carl Furillo, Ralph Branca and Gene Hermanski were having breakfast. They smiled at me and invited me to sit down with them. Until that moment, I had been a Yankee fan. They talked with me, asked about my school and "Would I like to meet some of the other Dodgers." They introduced me around and the Dodgers became my team – at least as long as they were in Brooklyn. When I told my father what I had done, he smiled. I think he was proud of me, though he wasn't much for saying so.

When it came time for me to go to school, my father learned that someone he admired – a Mr. Farthing – had sent his son Billy to St. Bernard's, so that is where I was sent. I was at first the only Jew in my class and probably in the school. Fortunately, Mr. Jenkins, the headmaster, who knew I was Jewish, took a shine to me. That he knew who I was and asked how I was doing gave me the sense that he was looking after me. His concern for me became explicit in my later years at St. Bernard's when he backed me for the school's highest honors and tried to protect me from some of the anti-Semitism that was prevalent at the time.

St. Bernard's was the first school I attended – no nursery school, no kindergarten. It was September, 1942. The world was at war. The school had been founded by an Englishman and almost all the teachers were English born. The school was so English that we were not even taught American history. We were taught only English history, but I had no idea that this was anything out of the ordinary. Without thinking about it, I became a total Anglophile. The Englishness of the school was influential, and I was receptive. I wondered if I could be an English boy. Better than being an American Jew.

St. Bernard's was also a Christian school where we sang Christian hymns and recited the Lord's Prayer every morning in assembly. I liked singing those hymns particularly "Onward Christian Soldiers" which was one of my favorites. I did not think about the meaning of the words for a Jew and why should I have? I was more Christian than Jew in terms of religious practices. I did not have anything against Jewish religious practices. But I had never gone to temple and was unfamiliar with the rituals and the doctrine. I had absorbed Protestant practices in school although I don't go to church any more – except when I am with my daughter on Christmas Eve to sing Christmas carols, another hangover from my time at St. Bernard's. Being a Jew for me has nothing to do with religion and all to do with ethnicity.

I went directly into first grade. My teacher, Mrs. Ashton, was like a warm, caring, older aunt. She was calm, soft spoken – "No yelling allowed" – and encouraging. She was interested in me, in all of us. By Christmas, however, she decided that I knew everything she was going to teach in first grade. So after the Christmas break, I was moved into second grade – not a promotion I wanted.

If Mrs. Ashton was kindly and warm, the second grade teacher, Mr. Sindal, was her polar opposite. On my first day, as I was walking into the second grade locker room in my dark blue coat and long red scarf – and my very long hair, Mr. Sindal threatened me: "If you don't get that hair cut, I am going to take a lawnmower to it." I was frightened – but I got my hair cut. "I want to go back to Mrs. Ashton," I wept. But I couldn't. The fact that I was now two years younger than my classmates had no effect on my parents' expectations: I was to excel – "be the best"– in sports as well as academics.

In third grade I got my first taste for politics. That spring we "debated" the merits of the candidates for president in the 1944 election. I was in a very small minority (if not alone) favoring Roosevelt over Dewey. My parents were Democrats, although to my knowledge they never admitted it publicly – their friends were Republicans – and I knew nothing of their political affiliations until many years later.

The fourth grade teacher, Mr. Spicer, was very strict, and it was in his class that Tommy Lumbard (the son of a very well regarded judge) walked out onto the classroom window ledge in protest. I didn't know what was going on but recall being terrified that he might fall. He didn't, but I don't think he came back the next year. In Mr. Spicer's class I was awarded a prize for the best cursive handwriting. The honor turned out to be a disaster, because I no longer tried to make my letters nicely. Instead I wrote fast and didn't care whether others could read my writing. My handwriting now is hardly decipherable.

It was also in the fourth grade that I learned how demanding my father could be about schoolwork. One sunny Sunday I planned to play ball with some friends in Central Park. I had a science exam the next day and, as I was leaving the apartment, my father asked me, "Do you know the material?" "Yes," I said. "Let's see," he responded, taking my yellow science textbook into the den. Sitting in his chair with his back to the window and the gleaming sun so I could not see his face, he started asking me questions. My answers were not good enough. Goodbye ballgame as my father started going over the material with me.

The next day my father asked how I did on the exam. I said proudly, "I got a 99, the best mark in the class." My father's reaction: "What happened to the other point?" And he wasn't kidding. As far as he was concerned, I had not done my job. Could I never satisfy him?

Not only was I expected to get perfect grades, I was also expected to excel in sports – an almost impossible task since I was two years younger than my classmates. The problem came to a head in the fifth grade. We had a fifth grade soccer team that played other schools. Everybody in the class was on the team. I was a substitute, the lowest rank. "Not acceptable" – didn't meet my expectations for myself, or my parents' expectations of me. Desperate to succeed, I hit upon a plan: after the season, I invited the best player on the team to come over to my house almost every Saturday for several months to play soccer in my room. (I have to thank my mother for allowing it. We didn't break anything as far as I can remember.) The next year I was the only sixth grader to be a starter (left halfback) on the school's varsity soccer team which was made up almost exclusively of eighth graders. I was "the little engine that could" – a nice feeling. My father's drive for success had succeeded in imbuing me with ambition. I wanted to please him, but that was only part of it. I had an ego as well. I thought I was good, and that there was no reason why I shouldn't succeed at whatever I tried. I might have to work hard, but I was willing. If I wanted it, I could get it. In that sense, I was just like my father.

In fifth grade, at age eight, I had a few experiences that gave me the sense that being a Jew was not acceptable. I wondered, "Were Jews somehow bad?" My best friend, who was also Jewish – there may have been a dozen Jews in the school now – and had the highest marks in the class (I was second), had changed his Jewish-sounding name to one that sounded completely American, and moved to the mid-west. (We have become friends again as adults. Yet when we reminisce about the old days, we never talk about being Jewish or our name changes and how we or our families dealt with it.)

I had also heard that there were no Jews listed in the Social Register – the "bible" which the families of several classmates kept on a plate in their front hall. When my classmate and friend, George Hatch, pressed me on my religion one day as I sat on the window seat in his room in his family's brownstone on 92nd Street, I tried to dodge the question, but finally I said, "I'm Jewish; you can throw me out if you want." It was a spontaneous comment, but it revealed the fear of rejection beneath my confident appearance. I don't know whether I really thought he would throw me out. His parents were good people who had been very nice to me on the weekends I spent with them in their country home. Maybe they thought I might be Jewish and that was why George asked the question. My answer did not change my relations with them or with George. Maybe they had some feelings about Jews, but what did that mean in practical terms? I never found out, and it was clearly confusing. Was I really a Jew? I was Jewish because I had been born to Jewish parents. I didn't go to temple or observe any religious holidays. Instead, I went to dancing class and to parties with elegant young people who seemed to accept me as a friend and classmate without asking about my religion. Maybe I could be whatever I wanted which fit my ambition to be an actor.

I think I was struck by the stage bug when in the second grade I got to sing "I've Been Working on the Railroad" in a class performance. From then on, all through grammar school, I was in every play, usually with the lead. In sixth grade I had been cast in a small part (the widow) in the eighth grade play *The Taming of the Shrew*. On the day of the performance, the headmaster called me at home to tell me "You are going to have to play Tranio - a major role -tonight because Wright Palmer is sick." "Wow," I thought, "That will be fun." Whatever my other problems, I didn't lack confidence. That afternoon I read over the script with my Uncle Walter, so I would at least have some sense of what I would be reading on stage. My practice paid off because the performance went smoothly except for one memorable moment which gave the audience their biggest laugh of the night. I was reminded of this 67 years later at a monthly black-tie dinner by a tablemate who had been with me on stage at the time - small world. The scripted line was "I am my father's only son and heir," which I read as "I am my father's only son and hair."

My first ten years – before our lives were transformed by the family secret – were hardly ideal, but when I compare them with the childhoods of many friends, they seem a lot better. On the whole, I was a happy privileged child. I loved my family. There were pressures, but I survived them. I liked being with my parents, especially on Sunday nights, when we would gather in the den, eat sandwiches on rye, and absorbed in our own thoughts, listen for hours to wonderful radio programs like *Ozzie and Harriet, Jack Benny, Edgar Bergen and Charlie McCarthy, and Fred Allen* that shaped the American dream and fed ours.

III.

The Family Secret

Anti-Semitism was rampant in America during the 1930s and 1940s. In Europe, Hitler-inspired persecution of Jews began with the loss of their civil rights and ended with the death of six million Jews after terrified, exhausted families were jammed into freight trains then gassed in Nazi extermination camps. Those lucky enough to escape the Final Solution fled to whatever countries would take them. The United States had strict quotas and required visas which were difficult to get. Newly arrived immigrants may have been greeted by hugely popular songs with lyrics like "Somewhere over the rainbow skies are blue, and the dreams that you dare to dream really do come true," written by earlier Jewish immigrants like Yip Harburg (born Isadore Hochberg), Irving Berlin (born Israel Isadore Beilin) and Harold Arlen (born Hyman Arluck), but the reality of life in the States was not that rosy. Of course, life in the United States could hardly be compared with death in Nazi-occupied Europe, but anti-Semitism was widespread, respectable, and as commonplace as white bread – in print, speeches and on the airwaves. The iconic Henry Ford sat comfortably in his office beneath a photograph of Hitler, and Charles Lindbergh, the era's greatest hero, spoke out against the influence of Jews while heaping praise on the Luftwaffe as a model of modern airpower. Clergymen and radio personalities like Father Charles Coughlin and Gerald L. K. Smith broadcast hatred toward Jews and support for Nazi racial and religious doctrine to large audiences.

Jews were openly unwelcome in social clubs and in many white-collar and professional positions. My first year at a white-shoe law firm, an associate who was Jewish told me, "They will never make a Jew a partner here" – and that was in 1965. (He was wrong; many years later he became the senior managing partner.) Jews were excluded from country clubs, exclusive suburban and urban neighborhoods and residences, and organizations and associations that catered to the powerful. When I was in my 40s, a cousin showed me a chain across the back entrance of a Westchester country club on which he said there used to be a sign "No dogs or Jews allowed."

Jews responded by establishing their own clubs and organizations for people willing to accept such alternatives, but my father was not one of them. Jewish quotas existed in higher education – 10% in every Ivy League school. These were not hidden policies. They were well-known, publicly declared. Anti-Semitism was respectable.

In this environment, it was hardly unreasonable for my father to want to conceal and lie about his Jewishness. He was not religious. He did not go to temple or celebrate Jewish holidays except when visiting his family. And, he had childhood memories of being terrorized and called "Jew-boy" and a "dirty Jew." He was more than able, and he was ambitious. He wanted success, and he needed access. To get it, he sought to join the upper class Christian establishment.

Changing his birth name of Arthur Edward Moskowitz to

A. Edward Masters must have seemed like a logical step. Name changes were not new to his family or to many Jewish families who wanted to appear less Jewish and/or more "American". His grandfather and his granduncles had each changed their names so that they would not be drafted into the Austro--Hungarian army. According to my cousin Allan Kluger, "Their ages were also changed for the same reason, or to get lower insurance premiums." That might explain why my father's birthdate is variously listed as December 8, 1904 and December 5, 1905. To support the name change, my father ripped a page out of a public register that linked him to his birth name. Did my father think about the ethics of a lawyer destroying a public record?

My father told me he changed his name before I was born, and that is why I responded negatively to every questionnaire that asked whether I was known by any name other than Jon Joseph Masters. My father had lied to me. Just last month, reviewing some genealogical research my sister-in-law had done, I found I was listed in the 1940 census as Jon Joseph Moskowitz. Digging further, I found a letter dated a month after I was born in which my father's co-counsel referred to my father as A. Edward Moskowitz. Since I was Masters when I entered St. Bernard's in September 1942, my name must have been changed between 1940 and 1942.

Perhaps my father wanted to protect me by obliterating the "baggage" of the Moskowitz name. Being Masters probably worked in my favor. But his disregard for the truth throughout his life colors all my memories. When was he telling the truth? When was he lying? Was it just to conceal his Jewishness or was it whenever it was expedient – or perhaps he saw them as the same? Could I ever trust him? What other lies had he told me? Could he never trust me? I wanted to be close to him. I admired him in so many ways, his smarts, his warmth, his independence, his confidence, his ambition, his elegance. Yet, he lied to me. I am not angry. I am disappointed. That was not the way I was going to relate to my children.

Truth was not a priority for my mother either. She was born on March 6th, but she wanted to have a summer birthday, so she told everyone, "I was born on July 12th" and that was when we celebrated her birthday. I was 67 when I discovered this deception. Her claimed maiden name, Shady, seems to me today ironically apt since my mother revealed what she wanted to reveal and nothing more. I didn't learn that her maiden name was Shaderowfsky (sometimes spelled without the "w") until I was in my mid-40s – and I learned it from a cousin. Had it been up to my mother, I would never have known.

My mother's true age was also a military secret: "That's none of your business," she said when I asked. I learned her age from her accountant when she was in her 90's. However, when I was in the 7th grade, I clearly remember her telling me, "I'm 25." When I repeated that at lunch one day at school, I was greeted with derisive laughter. She looked very young, and I was only 10 at the time, but clearly she was more than 15 when she married, and as it turned out, I wasn't even born until she was 30. Yet, I repeated it because I believed her.

I don't think she gave a moment's thought to how her lying might affect me. That wouldn't matter. But she too wanted to hide my Jewishness – whether for my sake or hers, I do not know. My mother wanted me to be seen as a typical Gentile, which in her view was a little Dutch boy – wooden shoes and all, the one who stuck his finger in the dike to stop the flood. She chose what she thought was a Dutch name "Jon" from a name book, but she must have misspelled or mispronounced it. "Jan" not "Jon" is the Dutch equivalent of my name the way my mother pronounced it. The nationality of Jon is ambiguous, which actually makes some weird sense given my Ukrainian and Hungarian heritage. Unknowingly, she had not chosen the name which would allow me to fully escape her Jewish background. But she kept trying. She dressed me in lederhosen at the height of the Nazi persecution.

While the name change was no doubt necessary to conceal our Jewishness, I had no idea that it would have any real effect on our lives. My father's two younger brothers, Sam and Walter, also changed their name to Masters. We were still part of the family – a large Orthodox Jewish family which rose to prominence on the shoulders of my grandfather's success.

My father did not embrace the family the way his siblings did, but as he once told me, "I don't want to cross my mother." Did he fear her or love her? Maybe both. It could be that when he was a little boy, she protected him from his father. He never said so, but that is my speculation. My father, the most financially successful of his siblings, saw himself as different from his brothers. He was not only the smartest, but the only one of the five sons to marry early or have children. He respected his oldest sister, Anna, and listened to – though sometimes rejected – her advice. She adamantly opposed his moving to our apartment which was on 79th Street because it was "too far uptown." He was supportive of his youngest brother, Walter, inviting him to the apartment, lending him money (which, according to my mother, was never repaid), and giving him business advice, which he probably didn't take. However, my father did not like answering to the family or involving them in his affairs. He married my mother without first introducing her to them

-a headstrong decision, as my parents knew each other only seven days before they married. But I don't think that was the principal reason for his behavior. My father was a loner who didn't want anyone telling him what to do. The only time I ever remember my father asking anyone their opinion was at the racetrack when he would ask the ushers, while they were wiping off his seat, what horses they liked. Did he ever bet on their choices? Maybe, because he always wanted to have a winning ticket, and he often bet several horses in a race.

I think he found the family suffocating. According to my father, the older siblings could and would tell the others how to live their lives. All boyfriends and girlfriends were scrutinized by the whole family and sometimes rejected. It was family above all – I wonder to what extent that was because there were not many Jewish families in the Pennsylvania area where he grew up. I also suspect he thought he was better than his siblings, so what was the point in associating with them?

My grandmother's death in December 1947 was a pivotal moment in my father's life and, by reflection, in all our lives. Shortly after her death in Scranton at 73 or 76, he decided to completely free himself from his Jewish family – actually, if metaphorically, to get rid of his siblings. He cut them all off – refusing to recognize their existence – except for Uncle Walter, who had also changed his name to Masters. He purged their pictures from the family photo albums. He did not want to have anything to do with them. Many years later, his brother Sam told me that about five years after my father left the family, he (Sam) was crossing 57th Street at Fifth Avenue and saw my father crossing in the opposite direction. Sam said he called out to my father, "Eddie," but my father walked right past him as if Sam wasn't there. There was no question in Sam's mind that my father saw him. That was my father. When he decided he was going to do something, he did it whatever the cost to his friends or family.

As my father had cut off his family I assumed that my mother had also cut off hers since I no longer saw any of them. I subsequently learned from a cousin that my mother visited her mother a number of times between 1947, when she had also vowed not to see her relatives, and 1977, when her mother died. I have no idea how often my mother saw her family. She never discussed them and I never saw them again.

As drastic as it was, changing his name and cutting off his family were not enough protection for my father against anti-Semitism. He decided not to be a Jew and joined the Episcopal Church. Many Jews converted, a few perhaps for genuinely felt religious reasons, others for social and business reasons. I am convinced it was the latter for him, but it must also have been affected by his experiences of rejection as a child, as "a dirty Jew." If he had any objections to the Jewish religion, Jewish culture, Jewish values, he never expressed them. Did he dislike Jews? I have no idea as he did not talk about them. I have no idea what his religious beliefs were – if he had any. I think he saw religion simply as a way up the social ladder. The issue for me was not the conversion – given my experience in the fifth grade, I could see the advantage of not being a Jew – but the way he did it: creating a secret that wiped out the family's past. I never knew if my mother just went along or agreed wholeheartedly.

I was sitting in my bed on a Sunday morning in the spring of 1948 reading the comics when my parents came into my room and sat down at the foot of the bed. "We're going to become Episcopalians," my father announced, with no preface that I can remember. "We are doing this for you, so you won't suffer discrimination. However, if you are going to avoid anti-Semitism, you can't ever admit you were Jewish. Therefore you have to promise never to tell anyone that we were Jews – not anyone – not any woman you might marry, and not your brother Kim who is in the next room in his crib – not ever. And if you tell anyone, I will die. Now, if you don't think you can maintain that secret, we won't do the conversion. We'll forget the whole thing. The decision is yours."

I was ten years old and don't recall having any emotional reaction. It was more like, "If that is what we should do, OK." Had my father thought through the consequences of what he was asking? I certainly didn't. My parents had decided the right thing to do. Did I have a choice? Why was he trying to make me responsible for the decision? Bizarre. If I had objected, would he not have done it? Never had my father given me such power, and I was sure he was not giving it to me now. If I objected, he would have told me I was wrong – that he knew better. So I promised with no understanding of the effect it would have on my life. I had no idea that maintaining the secret would mean that I would never, ever, be able to share my feelings with anyone other than my parents. I would always be a child, circumscribed even as an adult by my father and mother. I could never go back to the family.

My takeaway, several years later, was that I had to learn to protect myself. It was my life, and I could not trust that my parents or anyone – even with the best intentions – would make the right decisions for me. I had to think things through for myself. My life was my responsibility. In an odd way, that decision made me more like my father than I would like to believe: just as he wouldn't take advice from anyone because of his past, I too was hobbled by a lack of trust that would make it difficult if not impossible for me to act on the judgments of others.

My father had accepted Hitler's redefinition of a person's religion, using a racial label based on heritage rather than one based on religious belief and adherence. Lying about our past did not seem to be a problem for my parents because truth-telling was not high in their hierarchy of values. But was it possible to wipe out your past? My parents seemed to believe that saying something was so made it so. Reality was what you wanted it to be. Like his father, my father wanted to be in total control, "Order it and the world will obey."

That said, I nonetheless saw my parents as warm, sensual people. I remember my mother telling Rosemary, "A woman should smell nice." My mother was very aware of what makes a woman attractive, and I am eternally grateful that she took the time to teach Rosemary all that she knew, because Rosemary's family had given short shrift to such things. My father, despite his bombast, knew and appreciated elegant clothes and fine food and wines, and taught me to appreciate the same. My life as a child was not just about overcoming anti-Semitism and hiding my Jewishness. It was rich in material pleasures, fostered by my parents.

IV.
The New Reality

It's astounding, but my father thought he could begin life anew at 42 and arise like a phoenix with no past while he continued to live in the same apartment and to practice law in New York, for a time in the same office. For "insurance" and to protect the secret, he cut off all his Jewish friends and his Jewish clients, but they knew who and where he was. It made for some pretty awful moments. I remember going into a fancy restaurant with my parents – I can't remember which one – where Billy and Ginny Salomon, my parents' closest friends at the time, were sitting at a table in the front. Billy was the first adult I called by his first name. Billy got up to greet my father, "Ed," he called out. My father walked right past him with no sign of recognition. I was horrified, but followed my parents. I didn't know what was going on. I was too scared to even ask about it.

One of my St. Bernard's schoolmates, Harry Moses, the only openly declared Jew in the class, asked me what my religion was. I tried to avoid answering the question, but he kept pressing, so I said, "I'm an Episcopalian." "No, you're a Jew," Harry declared. "My uncle lives across the street and until last year was very close friends with your parents. Why are you covering up the fact you are a Jew?" I did not have an answer.

The next summer my parents rented a weathered shingled house in Quogue, Long Island, a modest but elegant summer outpost of the quietly rich. The house was a bit off the beaten track, but it was still Quogue an inbred conservative community: the same families came year after year and newcomers were not exactly welcomed. Nor were Jews. Catholics yes, but not Jews. The first month there I played with a neighbor my age, Michael Flynn, who came from a Catholic family of modest means, probably struggling to maintain a place in the community. One day he came to my bedroom door and looked at me with the expression of someone who had to deliver bad news but didn't want to. After a moment or two, he announced, "I can't play with you any longer." "Why?" "You're a Jew." He stood there. He did not know what more to say. "I like playing with you, but my mother says no." That was that. The word was out and I could not hide.

A similar thing happened when I went to visit a classmate whose family were well-to-do long-time residents and also Catholics. We played together for a few days, and one day as I was leaving, his mother came out to the porch. She stopped short and asked me, "What are you doing here?" Then, "You are not welcome here." My "friend" shrugged as if to say I can't do anything about it. He wasn't allowed to come to my house either. Catholics, like Jews, were subject to discrimination in some places, but not in Quogue. Maybe they were afraid that associating with Jews would bring down community opprobrium. I never mentioned these experiences to my parents, partly because I did not think they could or would do anything about them, and partly because that's the way things were. I would have to figure out how to deal with it myself.

Keeping the secret made it hard for me to open up to others, which affected my ability to make friends and led to a disastrous experience my last year at St. Bernard's. Because I was too young to go to Exeter when I finished eighth grade, I stayed at St. Bernard's another year during which I took some specially created advanced courses but for all practical purposes, was considered a member of the new eighth grade. I was appointed head monitor, captain of the soccer team, got the lead in the play, and won all the major prizes. I was hated by my new classmates – hardly surprising as I had taken all the honors that should have gone to some of them. I was ostracized. I was made fun of. I was not invited to join the "secret society" to which many of the eighth graders belonged, and I was excluded from their Saturday activities. Someone forged and posted a note on the school bulletin board saying that I did not want to be the captain of the baseball team. I was regarded with some justification, as arrogant, but this made me look like a real fool and I did not know how to defend myself. I don't know whether the incident was at least in part a reaction to my being a Jew – a fact some of the kids knew – or simply a result of my inability to temper my success with a degree of modesty. Even today I don't go to St. Bernard's reunions because I fear that I'll be ostracized or derided all over again.

These experiences were the exception; most of the time my parents got their wish - I was able to pass in the upper class Christian world. Growing up, I had been invited to my classmates' weekend homes and to all the dances, including the dinner parties that preceded them. While I was part of the group, I was conscious that my parents were not. They did not socialize with my friends' parents and in many cases, were not known to them.

There was nothing intrinsically wrong with my parents' desire to succeed, but they did not understand the rules of the game. Fitting in went beyond the question of religion: it was a matter of conduct. You didn't call attention to yourself. You carried yourself in a way that quietly indicated your expectation that you would be treated well. You never made a fuss. You never raised your voice. While I grew up with these norms, my parents had not. That summer in Quogue, my parents invited flamboyant friends, particularly two Russians, one of whom was supposedly a prince, to spend weekends with us. The Russians brought girlfriends, introduced as "models," whose ultra-short dresses and loud behavior on the tennis court outraged members of the ultraconservative, well-mannered, upper class country club. Not surprisingly, my parents' guest membership was summarily terminated.

In restaurants my father could be an embarrassment. He insisted on getting the best table, and if he didn't, he raised a ruckus. "This table is NOT satisfactory. I will not sit in the back of the restaurant. I want a table up front," he would shout. He berated waiters who did not give him exactly what he wanted. Woe to the waiter who brought him eggs not cooked to his satisfaction. Those were times I wanted to hide. Sadly, my parents never understood how upper class Christians really behaved because most of the people they associated with and used as models were not members of that group.

My parents were charming, intelligent and well dressed, but they couldn't socialize with the parents of my schoolmates because they knew my parents were Jewish. My parents' friends – all Christians – came from people they met at parties and dances, on cruises, and in business who did not know my parents had been born Jews. Enough of them became clients of my father's to support his thriving legal practice, though they were mainly people with inherited money and not much talent who needed someone to direct their lives – which suited my father fine. "I no longer respect my clients," he said, but he socialized with them well beyond his business needs. He arrived at my 40th birthday party very late, choosing to spend the evening with a client who asked my father to get call girls for him. I remember wondering where I fit in his priorities. But I didn't ask him. I just got him a drink and a piece of cake.

Others were transients and newcomers – like the former foreign ambassador who just landed in New York and the retired executive who had lived all his life in the Midwest. They were innocents with no understanding of the ways of New York society – fertile ground for my parents to take charge. After my father died, a guest at a party given by one of my father's former clients, then a client of mine, told me my parents were "quintessential old New York."

My parents regarded appearance, dress and, to a lesser extent, manners as the principal markers of class which they equated with worth. They immediately wrote off those who – regardless of their status or talents – did not look or dress in accordance with their view of what was proper. Typically, they greatly admired the well-dressed Duke and Duchess of Windsor as models despite their flamboyant behavior and support of Hitler.

My parents' fear of exposure and my father's need to be in control of every situation precluded genuine relationships with others. He was overly flattering to strangers and domineering to those he knew. Because my parents saw my brother and me as extensions of themselves, they believed that whatever we did reflected on them, and they were constantly afraid one of us would do something that would endanger their social position or "expose" the family secret. At the same time, they wanted to use us to help them realize their ambitions. Their difficulty differentiating their interests and lives from ours was obvious in my mother's frequent mantra: "You want..." never "I want", whenever she wanted us to do something.

In the end, my parents thought they had to control my brother and me – what we did, how we dressed, how we lived our lives – everything. They drove my brother nuts, criticizing him for having bulging pockets and for wearing his eyeglasses – eventually he had a breakdown. The fact that he had difficulty seeing without his glasses did not matter to them. If we did not do what they wanted, no matter how minor the matter – my parents had what can only be called a "shit fit". They tried to control everything and everybody around them. My father would not even answer the phone unless he knew who was calling and what they wanted.

I loved my parents, but pleasing them was never easy. While my father wanted me to study, my mother was always telling me to go outside and play rather than stay inside and read. Her attitude was doubly confusing because on other oc- casions she nagged me about my schoolwork – although her nagging seemed more directed to my status than my educa- tion. In my last year at St. Bernard's, I wanted a baseball bat. When she refused to get me one, I asked if she would change her mind if I won either the Scholarship watch for the highest grades or the Paine Whitney Honor Cup for the best all-around student. Her response: "Only if you win both of them." I did win both – and got my baseball bat – but the school had to make a special call to my father to get him to come to see me collect the prizes.

Mr. Jenkins, the headmaster at St. Bernard's, tried to protect me from some of the pressures and the anti-Semitism, but he was a stern taskmaster and sometimes I didn't do myself any favors. One fall afternoon in seventh grade, the class was told we could play in the park after we finished our homework. Stu Kennedy and I finished the homework very quickly and were ready to go. But nobody else was, and we wanted them to come with us. Stu and I then let the other boys copy our homework – which we knew was a real no-no – and we all went to the park. The next day Mr. Jenkins addressed our class. He was furious. He lectured us, told us our conduct was reprehensible, and announced a punishment for the class, but excluded Stu and me. He then turned to Stu and me and told us he thought we should be expelled. On reflection, he said, he would give us a chance to prove that we were worth keeping in the school. We were scared but vastly relieved and a year later Stu won the Scholarship watch and the Honor Cup, and I won them both the following year.

Mr. Jenkins saw to it that I had every opportunity to suc-ceed. Once when the coach took me out of a varsity soccer game against a rival school because I had been kicked in the shin and was bleeding profusely, Mr. Jenkins came up to me on the bench, "Get back in there. You're not hurt that badly. We need to win the game." He had overruled the coach, and he really made me feel good: telling me I was important to the team.

However, there was only so much he could do. In my last year, when I won the Scholarship watch for getting the highest grades on special exams given to the best students in the class, the parents of one of the other students who had taken the exams objected. I suspected that the objection was fueled my being a Jew, but it might partially have been a response to my winning too many prizes. The objecting parents were major financial contributors to the school and one of them sat on the Board of Trustees. Mr. Jenkins solved the problem by giving this other boy whose grades were lower than mine a Scholarship watch as well. While mine was engraved, his was not. I am not sure why I tell this story except that it happened and it stuck in my mind because I knew the other boy's mother was anti-Semitic.

At Mr. Jenkins' insistence my parents took me to visit Phillips Exeter Academy when I was 12. We toured the campus with a senior who spoke glowingly about the school except for the food which he said was "terrible." Later the Director of Admissions handed my father an application to complete and sign. I said, "Dad, don't sign that, I hear the food is really bad." My father immediately signed the application. It was a kid's comment and irrelevant to choice of school, but it was my way of trying to be involved in the process. He could have said, "It would not be bad if you lost some weight," or "I'm sure the food is not that bad," or something that acknowledged my comment. What stands out for me was that he completely ignored me – something he did quite often. What was I, as the saying goes, "chopped liver?" Only it wasn't a joke to me. There was something in his body language – an almost threatening manner – that sealed off further discussion and said, "Don't challenge me." Didn't I matter?

If I didn't, then he could drop me just the way he dropped his family. He scared me. The message was clear: "Don't cross your father." My mother didn't understand. She relished telling the story: "Jon thought Exeter was all about food." I am not sure why this particular incident remains so sharp in my memory, but it was typical of the way he could forestall any questioning of his decisions – or his authority.

I will always be grateful to Mr. Jenkins for convincing my parents to send me to Exeter – despite the bad food. I needed to get away – get away from people who knew I was Jewish and from the control of my parents.

V.

Away at School

At Exeter (1950-1954)

Exeter was a new world. After taking a family picture in front of Dunbar, my red brick ivy-covered dorm, my parents got in their car and left. It was a Sunday. I don't remember how I spent that night, but the next morning I felt freer than at any time in my life. I had no obligations, no assignments, and no classes until third period. I had two hours to do whatever I wanted. My father wasn't there to tell me to do something useful. My mother wasn't there to check out the clothes I was wearing. I walked around the town. I felt like a grown-up. I had a checking account.

My religion was not an issue. My classmates could not have cared less. My parents had arranged for me to be baptized and confirmed that fall as an Episcopalian in the local Episcopal Church behind my dorm. I went to confirmation classes for my formal religious training, and I am embarrassed to say that it did not make much of an impression on me. It was disrespectful to what I was learning and to those for whom it had great significance. I think I just went through the motions and did what my parents expected of me. To my parents being an Episcopalian was a way of getting ahead, not a belief system which you had chosen for spiritual or even intellectual reasons. I didn't agree, but they had inoculated me and I did not think about what I was doing. It was pointless to try to have a conversation – any conversation – with my parents, much less one over the way they were using religion solely to advance their social and financial interests. Church was required on Sunday and everybody went somewhere. I went to the Episcopal Church a few times and then switched to where my friends went: Phillips Church, the school's church, where the service was non-denominational Christian.

I was on my own at 13 with no support – no Mr. Jenkins, no parents – with just a bunch of classmates, most a year older than me, trying to establish ourselves. None of us knew who we were, although some of us thought we did. After all, I had excelled at St. Bernard's, won all the prizes, captained the soccer team, and had the lead in all the plays. I felt confident. I could be a leader.

Not so fast!

When the preps – first year students – who lived on the second floor of Dunbar gathered in the room next to mine to be briefed on the ways of the dorm, I suggested that we band together and elect a second-floor representative to the dorm council. My schoolmates liked that idea and said I should be the representative. What happened after that is not clear, but by the day before the election I had become a favorite to win a place on the council. That night, however, one of the other candidates put a note under everyone's door saying "Vote for King Jon." Needless to say I lost the election. Most likely, it was my arrogance – my armor against fear of disappointing my family and

*Me and my parents first day at Exeter in
front of Dunbar hall, my dormitory, 1950*

myself – that inspired my rival candidate's note. In any event, I had been taken down a notch in a flash.

To console myself, I decided to shine as a student – only to make another mistake. I was a smart aleck and lazy. When Mr. Vrooman, my first year English teacher, told us to write a paper on a topic on which I had written a paper in the eighth grade at St. Bernard's, I handed in my eighth grade paper. Mr. Vrooman put it up on the board as an example of how not to write a paper. Taken down again. My pride had been badly wounded, but I listened to what he said – I resolved not to be in that embarrassing position again.

I made a similar mistake in History class. At St. Bernard's, because we were graded on the questions we answered, it did not matter if we didn't finish all the questions. At Exeter, my first History test had two questions. I did a good job answering the first one, but I skipped the second one as unnecessary and got an E+, a failing grade. Once again my attempt to cut corners taught me a valuable lesson. I got A's on subsequent tests and won the year-end prize for Most Improved. It is a prize that still makes me uncomfortable because it felt like cheating. That was my parents' game and one I did not want to play. Had I known the rules from the beginning, I would have gotten a high mark on the first test.

Trying to win my way back through sports, I signed up that fall to play light-weight tackle football (those under 150 pounds). At St. Bernard's we played football in the park on Sundays, and no one could tackle me. At Exeter, I quickly found out I could be stopped, and when they put me on defense, I was too scared to make open field tackles. Another bust. The next year, I returned to soccer, but was assigned to a team whose coach knew little about the game and was just fulfilling a requirement to coach a team. Although my experience was as a center halfback, he put me on his second team as a left wing forward. I was not very good at that position, and when I couldn't do well at soccer, I lost even more self-confidence.

Theatre was my last hope for success in those first two years. I got several parts, some playing girls, but my reviews were never great. Given my acting record at St Bernard's, I was sure I would be a hot shot, but my classmates, also hot shots, offered far more competition than the kids at St. Bernard's. Establishing myself was not going to be easy. That "little engine that could" who went from fifth grade substitute to sixth grade starter on the varsity soccer team was going to have to rev up his engines.

Schoolwork seemed the logical place to start even though I took little interest in it - no surprise given my anti-intellectual upbringing. I dug in. Math came easy. If I needed 100 on a test, I could always turn to Math. Learning to write well improved my English grades as did the fact that I was adept at analyzing the books we read. In fact, the Harkness table discussions – at which students and the teacher sat around a conference table, listened to each other and expressed and defended their views – rebuilt my confidence: I was just as smart as most of my classmates, and smarter than some. In my third year a teacher offered me the opportunity to graduate in three years– an offer I declined; no way did I want to be yet another year younger than my classmates again. My brain worked. I just had to persevere.

In my third year, I got a helping hand from Stu Kennedy, my former St. Bernard's classmate, and now a class ahead of me at Exeter. We were soul-mates whose demanding fathers required that we excel - no excuses accepted - and both of us had been placed in situations where that was not so easy. We had been primed to fulfill our fathers' dreams. Stu, adopted late in his father's life, was dropped into the sixth grade at St. Bernard's with his father's demand that he be first in studies and in sports. Stu succeeded. I got similar pressure from my father with no allowance for being two years younger than my classmates and a Jew in a Christian school. Nonetheless I prevailed at St. Bernard's, and Stu was doing well at Exeter. But action begets reaction, and pressure begets rebellion though that wouldn't happen until college, where I became an even more arrogant wise ass.

At this point, however, I was focused on trying to feel good about myself, which I believed depended on my classmates perceiving me as both athletic and smart. Stu, who was the varsity soccer team goalie, got me invited to a tryout to replace an injured halfback. My club's coach could not understand why I had been invited, but he did not know what I could do. I beat out the boy who was considered the best halfback in the club system. Pretty good for a kid who wasn't a star or even a starter, but I got to play on the varsity team.

Stu was also business manager of the yearbook, the *Pean*, and asked me to join his staff. Assigned to getting advertisements, I asked my mother to put me in contact with her new friends who were officers in substantial business enterprises. They responded enthusiastically, and my reputation as a go-getter led to my election as business manager the following year. Winning over others who had been on the business staff longer taught me that hard work could bring success and satisfaction.

I was getting some recognition on campus as being a member of the "in" group though I did not see myself that way. A supporter, not a leader, I was reluctant to put myself forward, partly out of fear of exposure and partly because of my disastrous election experience as a prep. But I had no qualms about putting someone else forward and that became my strategy in Exeter politics. To elect a very smart, but not particularly popular classmate to the Student Council, I visited the rooms of students with whom I did not regularly associate and was surprised and pleased that they listened to what I had to say; in the end, my candidate won a seat on the Council with the second highest vote total – a win that added to my self-confidence.

Where there were ups, there were also downs. Despite the fact that I had leading roles in all the plays for which I was eligible, I was not elected an officer of the Dramatic Society. I was obviously not popular enough – at least with the theatre crowd. Deflating. What had I done wrong? I didn't know.

Even so, I had a good time my senior year. I had a group of friends – some of whom are friends even today. I viewed myself as competent; I was on the soccer team; I raised a record amount of money for the yearbook; and I got terrific reviews in my last dramatic role Tony Lumpkin in *She Stoops to Conquer*.

The big change in the reviews came from having had the opportunity the previous summer, 1953, to study at a prestigious school for young actors – the Lucille Lortel White Barn Theatre in Westport, Connecticut, where I learned the basics of "method acting." (One Sunday back at Exeter that fall, after we rehearsed a scene in which a drunk Tony Lumpkin is unsteadily standing on a table singing loudly and waving his arms, my fellow actors approached me worried that I was too drunk to go back to the dormitory. I was totally sober, never having had a drink – just acting.)

Agents regularly came to see us perform at the White Barn Theatre. When an agent wanted me to try out for a Broadway show, I called my parents to tell them the good news. They were not pleased. "No way. You're not dropping out of school for the theatre. You must go to college." It had never entered my mind not to go to college, but I was young for my class. I could have taken a year off. Besides, it was all moot if I didn't get the part, a long shot at best. Nonetheless, my parents had stopped me from trying. At the time I was upset, but in retrospect, it was a fortunate decision because while I was good, I was not great, which is what you need to be to succeed as an actor. It took me a long time to come to that realization. Not trying and not being willing to defy my parents, however, stuck in my craw and several times I tried to go back to acting later in life – even at one point saying I was an actor who was practicing law – which wasn't good for business.

Contact with my parents was limited to Sunday night telephone calls which I would make from the post office and in which I would reveal only what I wanted. My parents were interested in good news. Bad news was my problem, and I wanted to avoid their lectures. Even more secretive about their lives, they didn't mention that my brother had had a tracheotomy while I was at Exeter. I learned it from my roommate who by chance heard it from his parents when he was in New York for a weekend.

That senior year I believed the world was open to me, and by happenstance it dropped in on me, and I had the confidence to receive it. On a beautiful fall day I went to the yearbook office to ask my friend, Henry Olds, chairman of the yearbook, if he wanted to play catch, but he said he wanted to hear a presentation on how to get a NROTC (Naval Reserve Officers Training Corps) scholarship to college. I was not interested in the program, but Henry was determined to go and since he agreed to play catch afterwards, I went along. At the presentation, the Navy recruiter told an audience of probably 40 Exeter seniors that NROTC scholarships (which involved free college in exchange for one course a semester and three summers and three years on active duty in the Navy) were almost impossible to get. Well, that challenge got my attention. Even though I had no interest in joining the Navy, no one was going to tell me I couldn't do something.

So I applied, but instead of indicating eight college choices as required on the application, I put down only one, Princeton, where I was determined to go, which led to a telling exchange with a Navy psychologist. The psychologist, who kept me waiting 45 minutes while I could see him reading the newspaper, called me into his office and asked me two questions. "Why do you want to go into the NROTC program?" To which I responded, "I know I am going to have to serve in the military [there was still a draft], and the Navy is the best service and the NROTC program is the best program." "If you are so interested in getting into the NROTC program, how come you put down only one college choice?" "I am more interested in getting a good education," I replied. That was the end of the interview – much shorter than any of my friends' interviews. Despite or maybe because of it, I won a NROTC scholarship, one of only three Exonians to win one that year. Unfortunately, my friend Henry was not among the winners.

While most parents would have been delighted that their son had won a full scholarship to college, my father was furious. He told me that I did not know what I was doing. A week later he recanted to the extent of saying that he had checked out the program, and it was OK. Praise was not in his vocabulary. He believed that his job as a parent was to tell me everything I did wrong. What I did right would take care of itself. That approach may make some sense as an intellectual proposition, but its emotional impact was devastating: I could never please him so I gave up trying.

I bought in to the Exeter culture – *noblesse oblige* – *non sibi* (not for thyself). We were privileged but that meant we had a responsibility to look beyond our own interests. Helping others, trying to make the world a better place, was an obligation, not a choice. My classmate Jay Rockefeller (John D., IV) understood. One day during spring vacation in our second year Jay took me to Radio City Music Hall to see a movie, *Singing in the Rain.* We entered the theatre through a private entrance and were led to seats reserved for his family. Yet, back at Exeter when our group went out to Kurtz's for our regular Saturday night steak dinner, Jay's allowance restricted him to the tenderloin, while the rest of us ate sirloin. Not a great hardship, but it served notice that there was more to life than what you could get for yourself. Jay spent his life in public service. I, whose family never talked about public affairs and who had never given public service a thought, now began to think about it. At the time I had no idea that this event in the context of Exeter would be a spur for my later attempts at public service and for my desire to mentor and help others achieve their dreams.

There were times, however, when we chose to ignore the Exeter culture. We were teenagers, after all. One Saturday toward the end of the spring term our senior year, Mr. Roncalez gave our French 5 class a surprise test and walked out of the room. We, all seniors and some of the brightest students, rebelled, including Jay. We started openly discussing the answers to the questions. Mr. Roncalez heard us and returned. Cheating was an expellable offense, no questions asked. He had a choice. He could enforce the rules or he could recognize that we were good students who, a few weeks before graduation, had had enough. He lectured us and never reported the incident. It was a valuable lesson in discretion, in not following rules blindly, and taking all the circumstances into account – a lesson I took to heart.

At Princeton (1954-1958)

I was a cocky kid. I had survived and thrived at Exeter – on my own. I wanted to do things my way and I thought I could. Like father, like son?

I had not chosen Princeton after comparing it with other schools. I chose it because in the eighth grade Stu Kennedy's father took both of us to a Princeton football game where we saw Dick Kazmaier play at the beginning of his storied career – leading Princeton to a national championship and winning the Heisman trophy. After the game Stu's father took us to his eating club, Charter, housed in what I saw as a great mansion with wood paneled rooms and a pool table where Stu and I were invited to join in a game. I decided then and there I was going to go to Princeton. (Actually, in my senior year at Exeter I had second thoughts and made an appointment to see the Dean of Admissions at Harvard, but just before I was to leave for Cambridge, my roommate brought me a telegram from the Navy accepting me in the NROTC program at Princeton and that was that.)

I never discussed my college choice with my parents, but when I told them I had been accepted, they were pleased. "That's terrific," my father said, "because Princeton doesn't have fraternities." The penalty for being Jewish was always on their minds and fraternities were notoriously discriminatory. In fact, they were naïve. Princeton had eating clubs which everyone had to join in order to have a place to eat after sophomore year. Anti-Semitism was a factor in most clubs, and Jews were usually relegated to the "less desirable" clubs. By contrast, if I had chosen to go to Harvard or Yale (about 90 percent of my Exeter class went to one of those three schools), anti-Semitism would have been less important because only a small number of students joined their fraternity-like clubs.

I did not try to get the most out of Princeton for many reasons. I was tired of the pressure to excel. Exeter had been great, but demanding, and I wanted a break. Academics had never really interested me, and I did not work very hard. I didn't need to. At Exeter I had learned I was smart. I was also not very curious. I wonder if my lack of curiosity came from my need to hide my Jewish birth. I did not want people to be curious about me, and I wanted to be accepted. Although located in New Jersey, Princeton in some respects, was a southern school – some of my classmates were still fighting the Civil War and they hung Confederate flags in their rooms. It was NOT Exeter and religion *was* an issue.

I did as little work as possible in most of my courses - enough to do well on exams – but even less in my required religion course. (Religion was always a bugaboo for me.) The final exam consisted of two questions, both about St. Paul, about whom I knew relatively little. Before starting the exam, we were told to write our answers in separate bluebooks. I quickly figured that meant each question would be graded by a different reader, so apart from a few sentences I took a chance, answered both questions with the same essay and got what amounted to a B or a B plus. I was playing the system. My father would have been proud – had he taken an interest – but I was just being a smart aleck and missed an opportunity to gain a better understanding of the religious heritage which was playing such a large role in my life.

In my senior year, another classmate and I tried to see how few of the required readings we could read in our English courses – my major – and still get top grades. On the night before the exam, we invited the most knowledgeable student in the class to one of our rooms and plied him with beer while he told us what we needed to know. With this information, and by peppering our exam papers with discussions of other books by the authors we were studying, we got better grades than the student who had briefed us about the required readings. Our teachers were impressed that we had done outside reading and missed the fact that we did not do the work they assigned. Once more, being a wiseass undermined my education.

I was brash, and with confidence in my convictions, I laid it all on the line in the senior thesis, the most important paper I had to write; graduation and honors were solely dependent on how one did on the senior thesis and the comprehensive exams. (Course grades were irrelevant.) I chose to write on Mark Twain and show how, contrary to then current literary criticism, the basis for his mental depression as expressed in his later books could be found in his quasi-comedic early writings. "Therefore, all the previous critics of Mark Twain were wrong," I declared at the end of the paper with the assurance of a literary expert.

What I didn't know was that my adviser, whose main interest was the 17th century English poet John Milton, thought Twain was a children's book author and not a serious writer. My adviser had not reviewed my topic or read any of my drafts. Because I wrote well, he said he would just read the final version. He did not get around to it until a few days before graduation when he telephoned me to say he was giving me a failing grade. Unless another reader (required because of the failing mark) disagreed with my adviser, I would not graduate.

In desperation I asked my parents for advice. What I got was a lecture from my father, "How could you be so stupid? You couldn't choose a safe topic?" Once more, they had proven their interest only in what might affect them: at no other point in my college years had they inquired about what I was studying or commented on how I was doing. If I flunked out, I would not be able to open doors for them – that got their attention.

Fortunately, the other reader gave me an A, and I graduated, missing honors by a hundredth of a point. A few years later Rosemary showed me an article in the Book Review section of *The New York Times* praising a new book which came to the same conclusion I had, and was considered the first new perspective on Mark Twain. That was satisfying.

When I first got to Princeton, I thought I would make my mark in the theatre, but the results were mixed. My talent was limited. I started off with a bang – the leading role (Thomas Becket) in *Murder in the Cathedral* and as co-writer of the freshman show – but ended first year with a whimper, directing a play written by Charlie Fried which was reviewed as "Fried's little nothing." Sophomore year I was in the chorus of the Triangle show, *Spree de Corps*, which toured the eastern part of the country during Christmas vacation, though my singing and dancing were hardly notable, to say the least. I didn't have a musical ear so carrying a tune and keeping the beat were a challenge. The next year I successfully directed the highly praised chorus in *The Pirates of Penzance*, but one night filling in for an absent chorus member I almost destroyed a major dance number because I forgot my own choreography.

In truth, what I really wanted from Princeton was to join the establishment. I was like my parents. I wanted what they wanted, but on my terms, not theirs, and I was not a great success. "Bicker" was the period when upperclassmen visited the rooms of sophomores to decide whether or not to invite them to join their eating club. You didn't have to bicker in your own room, that is, with your roommates. I decided – my father would have approved – to bicker with those friends whom I thought more likely to receive invitations to the best clubs. They did, but I didn't. I am not sure exactly why I wasn't chosen, but somehow I couldn't connect with the upperclassmen who came calling on my friends' room. I was in trouble. I did not have a bid and bicker was soon coming to an end. Everyone had to join an eating club, and I did not want to be stuck at a bottom club. I went back to my room and talked to my roommate, my Exeter friend, Henry Olds. He offered to help, though I clearly did not deserve it. I had turned my back on him by choosing to go to another room to bicker. He had been invited by our old friend Stu Kennedy to join Charter, then considered the best of the second tier clubs. They banded together and also got me an invitation to join Charter. Some friends are with you no matter what. Henry and Stu showed me the importance of loyalty.

Whatever the cost, I still wanted to be part of the establishment. By junior year I was spending a lot of time with Charlie Chapin whose family were pillars of the conservative establishment. They had a large apartment just off Fifth Avenue on 79th Street, where they spent the winter months, and an estate in Far Hills, New Jersey where they spent the rest of the year. Charlie's father, a senior business executive, dressed for dinner in a formal red lounging jacket. Charlie and his brothers had all attended Groton, where the Roosevelts had gone for their education. I liked Charlie. We both liked the theatre, and that year he was in the Triangle Show, the touring musical. We went to the theatre together and talked about the plays at bars afterwards. On weekends he often took me with him to Far Hills, which was fairly close to Princeton. I went so often that his friends expected me to be at all their parties. I felt I was becoming part of the group.

I expected that Charlie and I would room together senior year. (Henry Olds had gotten married.) So, one spring afternoon during junior year I went into Charlie's room to have a conversation. He was sitting in his big chair strumming his guitar. I said, "We're going to room together next year, right?" He stopped, looked at me and said in as nice a voice as possible, "No. I can't do it." I was taken aback. "Why?" I asked. "I am going to continue to room with Kal [Ruttenstein, a Jew]." I pressed further. "Kal is interesting," he said. "You're nice but you're boring."

I was devastated. I had never thought of myself as boring! Would people really not want to have anything to do with me? I went back to my room and lay down on my bed. "What am I? I am nothing. I am worthless." I tried to think. It was true I did not fully open up to people because I had to preserve the secret. If I opened up – the only way an outsider, like a Jew, could really join Charlie's group – I would be breaking my pledge to my parents. Kal could be who he was: an interesting person and a Jew. I had to be "plain vanilla" or risk exposure. It dawned on me that my parents had created a catch-22. By hiding the past in order to get into the establishment, they prevented the openness which was essential for entry. That same fear about being open – and thus found out – had both limited my curiosity (was this what made me boring?) and led me to avoid situations where I was not sure I could protect myself. Looking back,

I should have challenged my parents then. Clearly, I wasn't strong enough.

Even though it was the middle of the afternoon, I went to sleep, which is what I always did when I felt bad or when I had to do something I didn't want to do, like writing a paper or studying for an exam. After an hour or so, I would get up and do what I had to do – perseverance was ingrained. I went back to Charlie's room and asked if he had any suggestions about whom I might room with. He suggested Johnny Todd, another Far Hills friend, who was looking for a roommate. Johnny and I linked up. Johnny's family was one of the most influential in New Jersey. Both his parents were delegates to the 1952 Republican national convention and influential in convincing Eisenhower to become the Republican presidential nominee. Despite their prominence, the atmosphere in the Todd home, a sprawling farmhouse, was casual – at least to my visitor's eye – and I was a regular visitor my senior year. While I was a welcome guest, I knew I was an outsider. I wasn't going to fool myself again. However, Johnny and I became good friends. He was a terrific roommate and the one who saw me off to the Navy.

Graduation from Princeton with
my parents and my brother, 1958

VI.
The Navy

I didn't want to join the Navy. I had joined the NROTC only because they said I couldn't. I had had enough pressure and demands to excel – being two years younger than my St. Bernard's classmates, maintaining the family secret, fighting off my father's attempt to control my life, dealing with the challenges of Exeter. Now I wanted to kick back, enjoy college, not march around a parade ground and take courses in boiler engineering. My moral compass was not well developed, not surprising given my parents' fecklessness, and I was much more concerned with doing what I wanted than doing the right thing. I had one of the best scholarships in the nation at the university of my choice and I was complaining. My Uncle Walter, who had fought on the beaches of Normandy in the Second World War, wrote me that "those who bitched the most often turned out to be the best officers." This comforting thought helped justify my behavior as a midshipman in the NROTC unit at Princeton: I was going to do the absolute minimum I could get away with.

I refused to wear my naval uniform all day as required on drill day each week, though I did put it on a few minutes before drill. On my midshipman cruise the summer after my freshman year, I came to inspection unshaven because I wanted a few more minutes sleep. The result? I was ordered to spit-shine urinals for two weeks. I co-wrote and produced the shipboard show, which I aptly named *Why Toilet Paper?* The senior officers in the audience were not pleased. In my junior year, we were required to do a project in engineering class. Because I did not want to build a boiler as most of my classmates were doing, I told the professor that I would like to explore the possibility of creating a yearbook for our Navy unit. He thought that was a terrific idea – at first. He wasn't so happy when, after researching the matter, I told him we would not have sufficient circulation or enough advertising to support one. He thought I had just gotten away with something. He was right – but I did do the research.

To top it off, I tried to get assigned to the London embassy rather than serve on a ship as a junior naval officer was supposed to do. Johnny Todd's family was a friend of our London Ambassador and asked him to write a letter supporting my request. Whatever he wrote did not do the job. Unthinkingly, I had adopted some of my father's attitude toward life: "Don't stand on line," and always look for the easy way out.

Princeton students who, like me, had won NROTC scholarships and would get a regular commission on graduation, had a reputation for being terrible midshipmen but excellent officers. If I was an outstanding example of the first dictum, there was no expectation that I would exemplify the second. The head of the NROTC warned the Navy Bureau of Personnel: "Midshipman Masters has the lowest aptitude to be a naval officer of anyone we have ever had in the Princeton unit. Put him on a large ship and watch him like a hawk."

As much as I was not looking forward to the Navy after

graduation, the Navy seemed equally uninterested in employing me. Three times Johnny Todd had to drive me to McGuire Air Force Base in New Jersey before the Navy found me a seat on a plane to Europe to join my ship the USS Northampton (CLC-1). We landed in Paris so early in the morning that I could not go directly to the naval command as my orders required. Passing the time while walking around Paris, I spotted a movie theatre showing *Bridge on the River Kwai*. I don't know why, but the movie moved me deeply – whether it was the determination of the soldiers to survive, their heroism, or what. Upholding their honor was more than a matter of appearance but the essence of who they were as military men. Putting on a uniform was not just a change of clothes. Suddenly, surprisingly, I began to think of myself as part of a brotherhood with values to defend. I walked out of that theatre proud to be a naval officer and literally strutted to the offices of the naval command. What a reversal! For the first time, I felt I was not just going through the motions, appearing to be a naval officer. I *was* a naval officer and that office represented something substantive – true values. I was astoundingly naïve to have been influenced by a feel-good movie. But the experience had awakened the unacknowledged idealist in me.

Unfortunately, that idealism did not last. I was put on a plane to Lisbon where I arrived to find that my ship had left for Lebanon, taking marines to land on beaches in what was expected to be a combat zone. When they arrived, they had to step around the beach umbrellas and over the sunbathers. So much for our intelligence and so much for combat. That was the closest I came to combat in my three-year Navy tour, and I wasn't even on the ship that went to Lebanon. Instead, I went to Estoril and gambled at the casino while waiting for the ship to return to Lisbon. When my ship did return, I reported aboard. They had no assignment for me. So much for my sudden desire to serve in the Navy, and the Navy's interest in me.

During my first few days aboard ship I was sent to the Communications division where I had a mind-numbing job decoding messages. Next assignment: second in command of the First Division, the deck-cleaning division, where they put sailors with no particular skills. The First Division officer was well matched to his troops, but my Ivy League background made me a poor fit. The wardroom, where the officers had their meals and relaxed, was equally unwelcoming and I had trouble finding common ground with most of the men --already career officers, or planning to become career officers. And I found even those who weren't entertaining such plans not very interesting. As we steamed back across the Atlantic to dry-dock for refitting in Norfolk, Virginia, I thought with some dismay, this is going to be a long three years – not an auspicious beginning.

Then chance took over, and my Navy career made a sharp upward turn. The first day in port, I was assigned as Junior Officer of the Deck on the evening watch. The Officer of the Deck was the Legal Officer, Lt. Jack Tomion, who was reputed to be a law unto himself. I had heard that he had done "outrageous" (for the Navy) things like going on liberty with enlisted men, but I had never met him. There was nothing much doing on our watch, and we soon began a conversation. "So you went to Princeton. Well, welcome to the intellectual wasteland," Jack said. "Try having a conversation about Faulkner," he added. I rose to the occasion: "What do you want to know about Faulkner," I asked. And so ensued a long discussion about William Faulkner's *Absalom, Absalom!* which led to our regularly going on liberty together to browse a Norfolk book-store. We became friends.

I could not understand why Jack was going to stay in the Navy after his tour on the Northampton. He was a Michigan Law School graduate and had been on the staff of the law review. He had opportunities, and given my view of the Navy at that time as largely populated with by-the-book conformists doing dull jobs, he seemed out of place. In any event, Jack decided that I should succeed him as Legal Officer. I guess he had the authority or the influence, because a few weeks later, off I went to Naval Justice School in Rhode Island for a few months, where I was first in my class -- a fact I made sure Jack knew by my frequent postcards.

Shortly after my return to the ship, a new captain came aboard, John M. Lee, "Squidge" to his friends. One of his first acts was to read through the personnel folders of each of the 110 officers aboard. When he came across my folder, the nasty letter from the Princeton naval unit commander caught his attention. "Midshipman Masters has the lowest aptitude to be a naval officer…" That letter could have killed my Navy career, and had the captain been more stiff-necked and rule-abiding quite likely it would have. But that was not Squidge. The letter piqued his curiosity and he called me to the bridge. The first thing I noted was that he wasn't wearing a hat. Navy regulations required everyone on the bridge to keep his head covered. Then he told me that he appreciated my "fine Italian hand" in the postcards I had written to Jack from Naval Justice School. That was an expression I was surprised to hear. Clearly, I was not talking to a run-of-the-mill by-the-book naval officer. Captain Lee was special, and different. He was very bright and did what he thought was right. If a rule made no sense to him, the rule should be changed. That made sense to me. We were kindred spirits and I became his favorite. What I didn't know then was that Squidge was a favorite of Admiral Arleigh Burke, Chief of Naval Operations and at the pinnacle of the service.

Becoming Squidge's favorite involved a good bit of chutzpah on both our parts. When he came on board, of 110 officers, only three were qualified sea-going Officers of the Deck ("OOD"). If one were sick or otherwise unable to stand watch, the other two would have to rotate four hours on, four hours off – an unacceptable schedule. In order to get more officers to qualify, Squidge decided that qualification would involve a written test which he knew I could pass. He then insisted I take the exam, even though I had only been on the bridge as Junior OOD three times. He believed that my becoming a qualified OOD would embarrass others into taking the exam and would provide him with more qualified officers. Nice idea if a bit risky for the ship I thought, but he was the captain. I did not feel ready to be the OOD. Given my lack of experience, I could hardly blame the other officers for feeling the same. On my first watch as OOD, which happened to be during dinner time, several of the officers – to demonstrate their lack of confidence in me – wore life jackets to dinner. That was a challenge I had to meet head on, or I would never be accepted as an OOD. Confronting the men directly would not work. Instead, I asked the chief steward to call me when soup had been served. When he did, I ordered, "Hard right rudder, all engines ahead full." Then, "Hard left rudder." The splashing soup did the job for me. A good number of officers had to change their uniforms, and the tablecloths bore witness. If the officers didn't love me, I had at least gained some respect. The message was clear, "Don't fool with me."

Jack and Squidge were my exemplars for how to succeed

in the Navy. If you were smart, you could have a lot of free-dom. The Navy was actually quite rational, but having allies up the chain of command was important if you wanted interesting assignments.

A year later I was the OOD as the Northampton sailed up the Hudson River on the west side of Manhattan. I was following the recommendations of the pilot we had brought on board to help us navigate. Squidge did not like what we were doing. He relieved me and took over the Deck. Within minutes, the ship hit a barge which promptly sank. A serious accident. Squidge was on the list to be promoted to Rear Admiral, but promotion boards do not look kindly at captains who sink barges. Since I was the Legal Officer, I was charged with explaining to the Commandant of the Third Naval District based in downtown Manhattan how it really wasn't Squidge's fault – or at least he should not be faulted for it. The latter course was the better op-tion. The story we sold was that the ship "had just brushed the barge" which was swinging outside its anchorage, and that no real damage had been done – the barge's value being insignifi-cant. The Commandant accepted the story and Squidge's per-sonnel jacket was not tarnished. That was good news for both of us: Squidge was off the hook and indebted to me. I had done a good job as Legal Officer, and if that was an incentive for Squidge to reward me, I was in the catbird seat. It was his op-tion. I understood the game.

Understanding, however, is different from succeeding. I had to deal with Commander Eastman, the Northampton Executive Officer ("XO"), Number two under Squidge. Commander Eastman resented the fact that Squidge seemed to rely more on my opinion as Legal Officer than on his as XO. After Squidge, promotion in hand, left the ship to go to Washington,

Commander Eastman saw an opportunity to put me in my place. He called me into his office: "You have been gambling with the enlisted men, and you put on an enlisted man's uniform and went to their club." I was guilty of the former offense but not the latter. I had participated in a running poker game in Gun Control in the bowels of the ship with the Fox Division technicians who were some of the brightest people on the ship – and the most fun to be with. Fortunately, Commander Eastman could not prove the gambling charge without the testimony of people who did not want to testify because of their own guilt, and no evidence ever materialized on the other charge which I had vigorously denied. I had gone on liberty with enlisted men, but I never put on their uniform or went to their club. Instead of taking disciplinary action, the Commander gave me the lowest possible rating on my fitness report without giving me the opportunity to challenge it. However, the report had to be signed by the captain.

Luckily for me, he didn't know what had what happened to the new captain, Bill Bowen, shortly after he came aboard, when we were in Palma, Majorca. Captain Bowen's driver had driven his car through the plate glass window of a restaurant while the Captain was in the backseat with a woman with whom he did not want to be identified. As the ship's Legal Officer, I was charged with handling any claims for damage caused by officers and crew. I settled the claim without ever revealing the Captain's presence in the car.

Guess what happened when Commander Eastman gave the Captain my fitness report to sign? Captain Bowen rewrote the report, marked me as outstanding and lauded my service. I had watched his back, now he watched mine. That was my first cynical reaction, but it short-changed both the Navy and me. On reflection, there were many other reasons Captain Bowen could have marked me as outstanding. The fact that I bailed him out obviously did not hurt, but I had been doing an excellent job as Legal Officer (I was seen as fair-minded by the crew), Officer of the Deck (I handled the senior assignments – General Quarters and Special Sea Detail), and Administrative Division Officer (I was liked and respected by my men who performed admirably for the ship.) I was delivering substance. The black mark against me was that I was too friendly with the enlisted men. Like Jack Tomion before me, I had gone on liberty with them, and encouraged them to realize their potential. I took as my assistant in the Legal Office a seaman from the Deck Division who by the end of my tour on the ship had applied to Princeton. He did not get in, but later in life he was appointed Superintendent of Schools for a district outside Chicago.

Admiral Burke called Squidge to Washington to head the Politico-Military Policy Division on Burke's staff. Squidge's loyalty to me hadn't ended, and he got me orders to come along as his executive assistant. Working in the Pentagon and on the staff of the Chief of Naval Operations was a big deal. Even my father acknowledged it. When I was stationed on the USS Northampton, I had been driving my parents' black 1949 Cadillac convertible with a top that leaked. When I was assigned to the Pentagon, my father took me to a car dealer on Park Avenue and bought me – his idea, not mine – a very expensive silver 1961 Porsche Cabriolet with red leather seats. The car said it all. I was a success in my father's eyes – at that moment. I didn't know what this assignment would bring, but working in the Pentagon as an executive assistant where my nights and weekends would be free definitely beat standing watches on a ship as a way to serve my time.

I drove my fancy new car to Washington and parked in the garage of the Arlington Towers where I had rented a furnished one-bedroom apartment I had found with the help of one of my Uncle Walter's World War II buddies. I was proud of the apartment, but when my mother came to check it out, she was offended by the color of the bathroom. I spent an all-nighter re-painting it before she left. She had come to Washington to help me decorate the place and buy some furniture, and I wanted to please her, to connect with her. I never stopped hoping we could bond emotionally.

The Arlington Towers was a popular place for Pentagon workers, both inexpensive and a short commute – at least to the Pentagon parking lot which was so large one could get a day's exercise walking to the building. I got my exercise that first morning.

My orders were to report to Op 61, the Politico-Military Policy Division of the Office of the Chief of Naval Operations at the Pentagon. The building's interior comprised five con-centric rings, A to E. E, the outside ring, where the most im-portant officials had their offices, was the most prestigious. I do not know whether this says something about the inner workings of the Defense Department, but in the Pentagon only those with offices on the outer side of the E ring could see the outside world.

I was to report to an office on the E ring. Depending on where you entered and your destination, it was sometimes shorter to walk to the center of the building and find the correct spoke that led to the E ring than to go around the perimeter. (In the center of the building there was an open space where one could sun and eat lunch.) I don't remember what I did, but eventu-ally, I found Rear Admiral Lee's, a/k/a Squidge's, office.

Squidge greeted me warmly, told me I was to be his executive assistant and that for fun I would get a chance once a week to brief the Secretary of the Navy and several admirals on the contents of the super-secret intelligence Webb-Lovett messages which I would be given clearance to read. He then took me over to the administrative office where I completed an ungodly number of bureaucratic forms. I was flying high.

When I returned to Admiral Lee's office on the outer side of the E ring, he invited me to sit in and listen to a meeting he was having with the officers on his staff. They were discussing the fact that Admiral Burke had to be briefed that night on an arms control paper being prepared by the Joint Staff, because the Joint Chiefs were going to vote on it the next day. The person in the division in charge of arms control matters was sick and no one seemed eager to go to the Joint Staff, give the Navy input, and then brief Admiral Burke. They all seemed uncertain that they possessed the requisite knowledge, and none of them wanted to stick his neck out – these were career officers who, understandably, did not want to screw up in front of the Chief of Naval Operations.

I had no such fears. I was not a career officer and I had read two books that touched on arms control: Herman Kahn's *On Thermonuclear War* and Henry Kissinger's *Nuclear Weapons and Foreign Policy*. I raised my hand - and got some puzzled looks. Squidge took a chance. Not that he had other options, but he had always believed in me (so different from my father.) He sent me down to the Joint Staff as the Navy representative. This was heady stuff for a kid, even if it was only for a day.

I found my way through the various corridors to the small Joint Staff conference room on one of the inner rings to which our discussion was relegated to join three colonels representing

the Army, the Air Force, and the Joint Staff. I was a newly mint-
ed Lieutenant junior grade – equivalent to a First Lieutenant
in the Army or Air Force – and considerably below the rank
of colonel. Everyone was polite, but somewhat baffled by my
presence. I could see them thinking, "Why didn't the Navy
send someone more senior and more knowledgeable? Didn't
the Navy care about arms control?" I didn't blink. I thought I
could pull it off if I focused on listening.

The Joint Staff representative explained the arms control
proposal that would be reflected in the paper yet to be drafted. We all made comments, the others more than me. I did a
lot of listening and found myself agreeing with the Army representative most of the time. (Incidentally, this was a pattern
that continued more often than not throughout my time in the
Pentagon representing the Navy's point of view.) The Air Force
representative and the Joint Staff representative, also an Air
Force officer, seemed to be in tandem. (I later learned that at
that time Air Force representatives were required to take speci-
fied positions regardless of their individual preferences. Army
and Navy representatives had more freedom to express their
own views on the issues.) After everyone had his say, the Joint
Staff representative said that he would get us a draft as soon as
he could but probably not before we had to brief our respective
service chiefs.

Late that afternoon I walked down the highly polished E
ring corridor, with the walls plastered with pictures of heroes
and paintings of battles, to the office of the Chief of Naval
Operations. I was floating.

I was led into the large conference room where the briefing would take place. Several officers were there ahead of me
– a number of admirals and some action officers who, like me,

would brief Admiral Burke on the items on the agenda. Unlike me, the other action officers were full Captains (four stripes) with an occasional Commander (three stripes). I had one and a half stripes. Was I in the wrong room? Surely some of them thought so. "Was I a special officer, a lawyer or doctor or such?" "No, just a line officer." They were nonplussed, but then Admiral Burke walked into the room and we stood at attention before being told to take our seats.

My name was called, but before I could begin the briefing, I was asked again whether I was a special officer, this time by Admiral Burke's chief of staff. When I answered, "No," his response was an astonished "Oh."

I started describing the arms control proposal to Admiral Burke. Half way through my prepared comments he said, "Sounds pretty good to me." Reflexively, as though I were back at the Harkness table at Exeter and not addressing the chief officer of the U.S. Navy, I said in a voice that did not expect contradiction, "No, Admiral, it's not."

We were about three feet apart. He was sitting. I was standing. He was in uniform. I was in civilian clothes. He was a four-star admiral. I was a junior officer. He glared at me and leaned forward, tapping his right shoulder board, "Are you telling me, *four-star* Burke, that I am wrong?" "Well, Admiral, you asked my opinion," I blurted out without thinking how I might be embarrassing him in front of a large number of subordinates.

What was I doing? This wasn't the Harkness table. There's going to be hell to pay. Just as these thoughts were buzzing through my head, I saw Admiral Burke swing around in his chair to address all the admirals who were sitting in the audience. "I don't know if this kid knows what he is talking about, but I want you to stick out your neck that way." I was speechless.

I expected to be crucified, which was what my father would have done. And here I was being praised for speaking up! I later learned that this was vintage Burke. What a leader, I thought. I was impressed.

Then he turned back to me and challenged me to explain. I laid out the problems I saw with the proposal. I was calm, straight forward and clear. He looked thoughtful. Dead silence, for what seemed to me an eternity. Then, he said, "I think you are right."

This was a world-altering experience for me. I could only think what my father would have done if I had contradicted him in front of anyone, much less his subordinates. He would have had my head, told me I was wrong, and never, ever agreed with me. Yet here was Admiral Burke, the Number One man in the Navy, treating me like an intelligent human being whose opinions were worth listening to. It did not matter that I was a kid with no special arms control credentials or politico-military policy experience. He was interested in the substance of what I had to say. I was blown away. I had always thought everything had to be a fight. Talk about speaking truth to power and getting rewarded. Wow! This Navy was not so bad.

The next agenda item was a briefing by another officer from our division, Commander Meigs, on a situation that had arisen at the submarine base, Holy Loch, in Scotland. Fear of making Scotland a target in a nuclear exchange had led to protests against our basing a nuclear armed Polaris submarine there. It was the first time a nuclear weapon would be beyond sole U.S. control. The question was whose finger was to be on the button. Burke wanted to know how our position was developing and the status of negotiations with the British. Meigs' answers did not give Burke confidence that Meigs knew what was going on.

I went back to my office. Admiral Lee got a call from Burke, "Take Meigs off the Holy Loch situation and put the kid on it." Burke didn't choose me because I knew more about nuclear arms than Meigs. He chose me because he knew I would find out what was happening and give him straight answers - a lesson that has stayed with me: substance is critical, form is not.

What a day! Squidge had to look for a new executive assistant, and I was now a full- fledged action officer! For the next year and a half, the balance of my active duty tour, I was given assignments way beyond my pay-grade. I was sent to the United Nations to try to convince Ambassador Lodge of the military viewpoint on an arms control issue. I failed, but it was nice having a pass to the delegates' lounge and sitting behind our representative as the U.N. debated the then precarious situation in the Congo following the assassination of its first democratically elected prime minister, Patrice Lumumba. Other assignments followed. Even though I was 20 years younger than most of the officers in the Politico-Military Policy Division, I was treated as an equal in getting plum assignments. I became a defense policy expert. I had found my sea legs in the Navy and had begun to move away from my parents' emphasis on appearance over substance.

I had a hard time getting out of the Navy. I had done so well that a number of admirals tried to convince me to stay on, offering me command of a small vessel and promising return tours to the Pentagon. They tried to convince me that this was the road to becoming an admiral. I knew it had been their road, but no one could know what rules might operate in the future. Further, I knew that while I did very well as the bright young man working for senior officers, I was not nearly as accomplished in winning the favor of my peers who would be making the decisions about how high I could rise in the Navy. Although I had never thought of the Navy as a career, it was one of the most defining and rewarding experiences of my life –and totally unexpected.

As a Naval officer aboard the
USS Northampton (CLC-1), 1958

VII.

Getting Married

Even though I did not want to stay in the Navy, I very much wanted to stay in the Pentagon working on defense policy issues that were often in the press. The Pentagon was a hot bed of "whiz kids" attracted by the glamor of the Kennedy administration, which had taken office that year, 1961, and I had made friends with some of them. I had a good reputation, and they suggested positions where I could continue to work on defense policy as a civilian. I liked living in Washington. I was shuttling between debutante parties with attractive young women at the Chevy Chase Club and dinner parties in Georgetown with striving young men three or four levels below the Cabinet discussing foreign, defense, and economic policy and domestic politics. Washington seemed like the center of the world, and I felt like I belonged. I liked my friends, military and civilian, and since I was 10 or more years younger than most of them, it was like having a lot of older brothers who took an interest in me and from whom I could learn. I didn't have to worry about my family. My parents were not only hundreds of miles away, they had no interest in public policy so stayed out of my hair.

Life was good. Life was exciting. I had agreed to take a

short-term job with the Under Secretary of the Army immediately after I left the Navy – working with Gardner Ackley, then chairman of the economics department at the University of Michigan and later head of the President's Council of Economic Advisers, to determine the feasibility of a sea-level canal through Nicaragua. The thinking was that the locks in the Panama Canal were too vulnerable to military attack or sabotage, and that a sea-level canal through Nicaragua could be created rapidly using nuclear explosions. Gardner Ackley was to focus on the economic effects, and I on the politico-military effects, of the proposal. Before I did that, however, I had to finish my tour of duty in the Navy.

I certainly didn't think going to a football game would change my life, but life is rife with unintended consequences. By prearrangement, I met my friend Henry Olds at the Princeton-Yale football game in New Haven. At dinner afterwards, he tried to persuade me to go to graduate school, any graduate school, rather than work in the Pentagon after I left the Navy. He thought I needed to have a particular expertise because specialization was the "wave of the future." Having no success at dinner, he asked me to come back to Cambridge with him where he was teaching at the Harvard Graduate School of Education. I complied, and that gave him more time to press his point. Finally, at about 4 AM, I surrendered, "If I agree to apply to a graduate school, will you let me go to bed?"

Once back in Washington, I sent away for applications to Harvard, Columbia and Yale law schools. In my last year at Princeton, like many of my classmates, I had taken the aptitude tests for both law and business schools and because I had scored slightly better on the law exam, I decided to apply to law school.

The applications all arrived the same day, just as I was dressing for a cocktail party. Yale and Columbia each wanted an essay explaining why I wanted to go to law school. Too much trouble, I thought, to explain why I wanted to do something I didn't really want to do. I threw their applications in the wastebasket. Harvard just wanted permission to get my grades. I sent the application to Harvard and a postcard to Henry saying I had done the deed. I thought that was that. But ten days later I got a letter from Harvard Law School congratulating me on having been admitted. What now?

Well, in one sense, the choice was a no-brainer: my civilian friends in the Pentagon were Harvard graduates and JFK was filling his administration with Harvard graduates. They said I had to go, but that raised two problems.

For the past three years I had been on my own, living my life without interference from my parents, and I liked it. Now I would have to ask my father for money and even worse, I feared that would mean more battles because I would be studying law – my father's own field of expertise – and it was highly likely that he would try to control me claiming to know better what was best for me.

Swallowing my fears, I asked my father if he would pay for law school with the understanding that I would in no way be obligated to practice law. He agreed – not, I think, because my Navy ROTC scholarship had paid my Princeton expenses – but because he thought that law might bring us closer and make me more willing to accept his judgment about how I should live my life. I also believe he wished he had had the opportunity to go to Harvard Law School – again he was living out a fantasy through me.

On the Wednesday before Thanksgiving of our first year in

law school, I met Rosemary Cox when she turned around in her seat during the break between Contracts class and Property class to talk to Judy Wilson (now Judge Judy Rogers of US Court of Appeals for the District of Columbia). Since I happened to be sitting next to Judy, she introduced us. Rosemary and I went for coffee which led to our first date – a memorable dinner at the Boston restaurant Charles, followed by a play where from our seats on the top balcony we could barely see the actors, much less hear them. We almost froze driving back to Cambridge because we could not find the heat control in the Volkswagen we'd borrowed from a classmate (my Porsche was in the shop) and we got lost. Nonetheless, the evening was a success, and we made a second date

On our second date, the night before Christmas vacation, at a Greek restaurant in Boston with belly dancers, Rosemary bluntly told me to get lost. "You're not right for me," she declared. "You are not an intellectual." At the time I did not understand what that word meant to her. It seemed to me she was accusing me of being an uneducated boob. Insulted, I defended myself by pointing to the volumes of Faulkner, Hemmingway and Shakespeare I had read – obligatory college reading to be sure – and could discuss in depth.

I later came to understand that Rosemary came from a family that prized intellectual curiosity. When she was growing up, the family gathered around the dinner table every night to share things learned and ask questions. Unlike my father, hers was almost invariably present. They talked about a wide range of subjects: ethics, biology, psychology, religion, and pondered together about the underlying structure of things. They discussed rather than argued and were open to differing perspectives (except when it came to sex and politics – subjects about which they could be quite rigid). Rosemary has fond memories of times when she would ask a question for which no one had an answer. Together, she and her father would climb the stairs to a cozy sitting room where her father would show her a globe or pull out volumes of the Encyclopedia Britannica. Together they would try to find answers to her questions. "Who was Guy Fawkes?" "What caused the ice ages?" "What is gravity?" "Why don't things fall off the world?" Sometimes her father would say, "We just don't know. Maybe someone will figure it out someday." It can't be a coincidence that I, from a family that suppressed curiosity, fell madly in love with this lively, young woman who never stopped asking questions.

Rosemary was right – but only in part. I was not an intellectual, but I believed I was *right* for her. I was smart, I was kind, and I could not be cowed. My sense of social justice – Exeter's *non sibi* training – resonated with her beliefs – she had grown up in a Quaker community. Besides, I liked her. She was smart and determined – and warm, exuberant, and pretty – although in need of a good haircut. I wanted someone who could challenge me. She didn't know what she was doing, blowing me off. When I got back to New York, I wrote her a letter: "You don't know what you are talking about. You can't put people in boxes. They're much more complicated." Her response was an invitation to visit her home in Swarthmore, Pennsylvania for New Year's weekend. Although I did not know it at the time, her quick and favorable response was sparked by her recognition that I would not be intimidated by her – her essential criterion for a husband.

The first night there I spent some time talking with her father, who afterwards told Rosemary that I was very smart, by which her father probably meant that I had a highly developed practical intelligence. He may have regretted those words, which Rosemary took to mean that I was an intellectual, because they removed her principal objection to our relationship. Although her father respected my intelligence, I doubt I was what he had in mind as a husband for his daughter.

On the surface and based on our family experiences, we were a most unlikely match. Rosemary was a small town girl; I was a big city kid. Her parents and her brother were all academics. Her father, one of the founders of the science of marketing, was chairman of the Marketing department at the Wharton School of Business at the University of Pennsylvania; her mother had created and directed the child development program at Bryn Mawr College, and her brother was a professor of bio-chemistry at the University of Texas. Although my father was very smart, my parents were poorly educated and uninterested in ideas or any intellectual pursuits. Rosemary's brother's advice to his sister, "You can't escape who you are," was an implicit warning that we were not a good match.

But we were in love. Rosemary thought me warm, kind, handsome, playful and willing to challenge authority. To her, I had the manners of an upper class WASP and the emotional warmth and sensibility of a Jew – although at the time she would not have made the Jewish connection because she had not known many Jews. I thought her smart, pretty, warm, determined and sexy.

We had more in common than appeared on the surface. Both our parents were outsiders – mine as Jews and Rosemary's as Texans living in the northeast. We both wanted to become part of the power structure and "make a difference." We were both more confident in our ability to rise in a meritocracy than through the social class system. Rosemary knew there was a world of power, privilege, sophistication and elegance, but she was not sure how to reach it. I inhabited that world under false pretenses. I needed to solidify my base. We each thought the other could help us achieve our goals. Rosemary saw my Exeter and Princeton credentials, my ability to rise in Washington policy circles, and my parents' Park Avenue apartment as a way to the world she wanted to enter. My ambition, I told her, was to be Secretary of State. I wanted a smart, determined partner, and I figured anyone able to hold her own as one of 19 women in a class of 550 at Harvard Law School could thrive in any environment. We were engaged two and a half months after we met and married four months later.

While it did not derail our marriage, Rosemary's parents were politely anti-Semitic: her father complained that "Jews had taken over the University of Pennsylvania," and advised Rosemary not to go to Radcliffe because it had "Too many Jews." And her mother exclaimed, "It's so nice to see all those Anglo-Saxon faces" at the University of Texas football game. Their anti-Semitism struck a discordant chord with me, but never became an issue for her parents, because as far as they knew, my family and I were upstanding members of St. James Episcopal Church.

My parents were not happy about my marriage. My father, in his usual unrealistic and naïve way, wanted me to marry a "Rockefeller", or some other scion of the establishment, whose social distinction would help me – and therefore my parents – join the upper class. He specifically did not want me to marry Rosemary, who not only lacked those credentials, but also was smart – smart enough, I think he feared, to figure out that we were Jews. I was not moved by my parents' concerns, but I did want the approval of my brother, Kim. Before I finally proposed to Rosemary, we drove down to Choate, where Kim was in boarding school, so that he could meet her. He gave a "thumbs up."

My brother and I had not been close growing up. I was nine years older, and in fact, my parents had set us against one another. He didn't know the secret. He was told everything I did right and he did wrong, and I was told everything he did right and I did wrong. Both of us had been subjected to this nasty game and like most people who suffer a trauma together, it had the perverse effect of bringing us together. I did not want to lose him. I wanted a brother. He was my family and I did not want to cut him off the way my father had rejected his siblings. And I don't think Kim wanted to lose me because he saw me as his protector: why else would he have burned my suitcase when I was leaving Princeton for the Navy? It was an odd thing for him to have done, and I had not seen it as a plea for help at the time.

My mother saw that the marriage was inevitable despite her opposition and did not want to lose a son. She knew I was stubborn so she tried to make the best of it by building a relationship with Rosemary, helping her shop for clothes, seeing that she got a good haircut, and introducing her to sophisticated New York life as my mother knew it, just as she had done for a number of her less sophisticated friends. She also arranged for us to have a week's honeymoon in Bermuda. My father, however, clung to his resentment at having been overruled. I doubt he would have showed up at the wedding if it were not for my mother, and when he did show up at the bridal dinner, he was unshaven in protest – the only time I ever remember him with stubble on his chin and cheeks in public.

Despite their misgivings, my parents were generous. They

paid for our apartment in Cambridge, and for most of our daily expenses. Rosemary's parents paid her Harvard Law tuition. Other costs became my responsibility once I had married their daughter, a fair and unexceptional arrangement at the time. My parents also paid the bills when we visited New York: we went to places that we would never have been able to afford on our own, although most of the time we went with them. While they always wanted to know what we were doing at Law School and never shy about telling us about what else we should be doing, my relationship with them was going surprisingly smoothly – which was more than I could say about my relationship with Rosemary.

Dr. Pitney Van Dusen, who married us, accurately perceived the problem created by the secret in his talk with Rosemary a few hours before the wedding. I don't know how he knew because he had met me only once or twice, but he saw something that Rosemary had not seen: "Jon has not separated from his parents," he said. I was locked in by my pledge to keep the secret of our Jewish past. I had promised never to tell anyone else, and there was a part of me that half- believed that my father would die if I broke it. That meant I could not tell my brother or Rosemary. I had tried to get around this carpet of broken glass by asking Rosemary when we were courting whether it would make any difference if I were a Jew. She said, "Of course, not," but she heard the question as purely hypothetical. I am ashamed to say I never thought about the effect of my lies on Rosemary and Kim – the choices they might have made had they known the truth. The harm I was doing them. It was about me – protecting myself by preserving the family secret and not risking the consequences of the truth. Dr. Van Dusen was dead on.

I couldn't be open, and after a while Rosemary began to realize that something was missing between us. I was withholding something. I kept denying it. The more Rosemary pressed, the more I withdrew. It became a dreadful suspicion, then a threatening rift in our marriage.

But the problem was more far-reaching than the secret, though that was obviously the heart of the matter, as was my unwillingness to cut off my parents as they cut off theirs. The conflict that burst through the surface was one Rosemary sensed on our second date, without understanding the cause. The way I had protected myself against my parents' control was to fight back. Conversation was, for me, combat. My father would tell me what to do, and if I did not agree, I would have to beat back his arguments. There was a winner and a loser in every encounter. There was no such thing as a reasonable discussion of an issue where we could express our opinions and arrive at some negotiated conclusion – typical in Rosemary's family except if the subject was Vietnam. When I think of the effect of my combativeness and lack of curiosity on my ability to have an intellectual discussion, it is no wonder that soon after we were married Rosemary threw six water glasses against the kitchen wall in anger and frustrated disappointment at my resistance to discussing issues over which we disagreed. I had misrepresented myself. I was not an intellectual no matter how many books I had read.

But that outburst was the exception. The storm blew over, and for the most part we had a good time in law school. We made lifetime friends whom we enjoyed entertaining in our small apartment at the top of the stairs – no door – on the third floor of 48 Concord Avenue. We studied hard enough to get reasonable grades, worked summer jobs first with the government in Washington and then with law firms in New York, and made do on a tight budget. It was fun, but we had little time to really get to know each other. No real vacations free from the pressures of school, jobs, and parents.

It was important to our marriage that we had that time to enjoy each other free of other concerns. Our one-week Bermuda honeymoon was too short and probably too soon. We needed have some sense of what our life would be like when we got back home. I suspect what was true for us is true for other couples as well. We sold the Porsche and planned to sail for Europe on the *Queen Elizabeth* as soon as we finished the July bar exam. But opportunity intervened. I was offered and accepted a position on President Lyndon Johnson's Special Political Research staff for the 1964 election campaign which ended the first Tuesday in November. (Johnson had become President the previous November when President John F. Kennedy was assassinated.) It wasn't until November, 1964 that we took a vacation that was – and remains – a special time for both of us.

We traded our summer third class tickets for first class accommodations on the *SS Cristoforo Colombo*, and set sail for Europe. We had two months before we had to report to our law firm jobs, and with luck and thrift the money would last. We were on our own and living in the moment. Parents and secrets vanished from our minds. The paneled bar and entertainment area were inviting as was the pool, though swimming would have to wait until we were in warmer waters. Entering the dining room – casual but elegant – we found our assigned table.

We lucked out. We had been seated with Mary McGrory, a senior political reporter with The Washington Post, Adey Horton, a World War II English spy and devotee of George Eliot, and a concentration camp survivor, now a Canadian shoe manufacturer, and his wife. Conversations were lively about world affairs, politics and World War II. Everyone had interesting stories – personal anecdotes – and Rosemary and I were enthralled. The awful experiences of the concentration camp survivor were particularly vivid. One lasting effect of imprisonment was his yearning for rich desserts – just "feathers" he would say. He always ordered multiple desserts and insisted that we have them, too. Here was a Jew who was not embarrassed about being a Jew. He was proud and grateful to have survived the Holocaust. The others at the table were impressed, or so they said. I was impressed, but did not say so. My father had taught me to hide emotional responses, and for the moment I was uncomfortable.

Both Mary and Adey took a shine to us as an attractive interesting couple. They wanted to be with us on the ship and to join them in Italy and France. We had made no plans and had no itinerary. We knew the ship landed in Naples but we hadn't decided where to go from there. Mary wanted us to go with her to Rome. Here was this renowned journalist asking us, a couple of recent law school graduates, to accompany her! It gave us a lot of confidence and a great opportunity for us to learn.

Mary knew the ropes and made sure they were taken down for us. At her fancy hotel just off the Via Veneto she insisted we be given a room even though we did not have a reservation and the hotel was supposedly full. "Of course, Miss McGrory" was the manager's quick response. She was, however, less happy when the room clerk gave us a better room than hers because the clerk thought that Rosemary, who was wearing a loose dress, was pregnant. She wasn't.

That night Mary took us to the Abruzzi restaurant famous for their green lasagna and we learned what really good lasagna tastes like. I have never been able to find another restaurant that could do lasagna as well, though I keep on looking and hoping. Mary was determined to teach us the joys of Italian cuisine. She took us to a family restaurant around the corner from the hotel – not one of those highly recommended expensive restaurants – and ordered *zuppa de verdure*, basically a soup made from all the week's leftovers. It was so good we came back twice more. Again, I have never found a soup as good.

We were so relaxed that on our second day I got Rosemary to play touch football on the shores of Lake Nemi, south of Rome. The Italians had called a one-day strike so Mary had arranged for us all to picnic and play touch football with Senator Eugene McCarthy's top aide when Senator McCarthy was in town for the Second Vatican Ecumenical Council (Vatican II). The upshot, of course, was that we got invited to the opening ceremony to see St. Peter's in all its glory as the leaders of the church paraded down the aisle carrying the pope in his chair. I only wish that our Latin had been good enough for us to understand what they were saying. But the ceremony had a majesty we will not forget.

Neither Rosemary nor I had been to Rome before and we wanted to see as much of the antiquities as we could, especially the Forum. Mary found us a guide who had written his PhD dissertation on the Forum. Unveiling its history as we clambered up and down the stone tiers was for him a matter of love, and we were the lucky beneficiaries.

Mary knew scores of people – mostly ex-pats and newspaper people. They were lively and interesting and apparently they thought we were interesting enough because one invitation led to another, climaxing in a three-hour country meal at an ex-pat's charming apartment. Rome was a city for walking, and we walked everywhere. Driving was treacherous. I particularly remember strolling along the banks of the Tiber struck by its colorful history.

From Rome to Paris where Rosemary had never been. I did not know what she expected, but I knew Paris was not going to play second fiddle to Rome, and Adey made sure it didn't. He met us at the station and booked us into the Hotel de L'Universite´ where Hemingway had been a regular. Adey knew I was a Hemingway fan, and when the hotelier gave us Hemingway's large, high-ceilinged room with its own balcony, I was thrilled.

Rosemary wanted to learn about French cooking and Adey accommodated. That night after a glass of wine at Adey's book-lined apartment on a back street, we had a magnificent pigeon dinner at Nino en Clos (sp?) which we washed down with the new Beaujolais which had just arrived in Paris that day. From the restaurant we drove to the city's bustling central market Les Halles. As we walked through the marketplace, the produce began flooding in on trucks, and we began to feel like Parisians. We found a bar and downed our third bottle of Beaujolais. Time to go home. But on which of the streets leading to Les Halles had we parked the car? None of us could find it in our inebriated condition. Rosemary and I went home on the Metro. I don't know how Adey got home. But it was a fun evening and Rosemary's introduction to Paris.

Adey wanted us to meet his World War II buddy, Rene´ Chambrun, a descendant of Lafayette, who, according to Adey, liked to talk to Americans. That was fine by us although we were not sure what we were supposed to talk about. I remember Rene´'s office, a corner room with dark green walls lined with bookcases and historic pictures, and furnished with antiques,

on the second floor of what must have been a landmark building. I don't remember what we discussed, but he must have
enjoyed the conversation because at the end of our meeting
he told us he was also part owner of Baccarat, the fine French
crystal emporium, and gave us a card entitling us to a discount
which we used for many years thereafter for special occasions.
I think Adey hoped that was the way our visit would turn out.

Now there was time to enjoy Paris on our own. We wandered
the streets, walking everywhere. We wanted to inhale Paris. I
had been there before - on a bicycle trip after high school - but
never with someone with whom I could really share the experience. We went to most of the museums and as many concerts
as we could afford. Paris was filled with music, particularly in
the churches. We peered in shop windows and found treasures
– our best china and a turtleneck sweater that Rosemary wears
to this day. There were trips to Versailles, Chartres, coffee bars,
and when we craved a simple meal, The American Drugstore.
Oh, to be young and in Paris.

I wanted to take Rosemary skiing. She had never skied, and
I wanted her to learn so that we could do it together. Before
we left the States, I had made reservations in St. Anton. As we
prepared to leave Paris, not a snowflake was to be seen, but
the gods were smiling and when we arrived in St. Anton, the
first snows were falling. We did not have much money, but it
did not cost much to stay at a lodge a few yards from the tow.
Rosemary was hardly a natural, but with the encouragement
of her instructor whacking her behind the knees and shouting
"kniebiegen" (*"bend your knees"*), she learned to ski, and we skied
together.

A week later, it was on to London and Savile Row tai-
lored suits, courtesy of my mother who was always concerned

that I dress well; roast beef at Simpsons; Westminster Abbey; the National Portrait Gallery; the English Speaking Union; Christmas in Clovelly in North Devon with Lord Asquith's granddaughter and Sir Malcolm Sargent; and New Year's Eve in Trafalgar Square. Memories that bring me joy today. We were young and the world was ours.

We did not realize it at the time, but memories of that trip - our capacity to have fun together and to share our esthetic sensibilities – joy in the museums, the architecture, the history and the food - along with our shared experiences accumulated over time would sustain our marriage when we were at odds with one another. Conflict was inevitable. We were both strong willed. We would disappoint one another. In the beginning there was the family secret and my lack of intellectual curiosity. Other conflicts would follow. But just when it seemed we had come close to a breaking point, we would step back and think about how much we loved each other, how much we had shared, and how lucky we were to have found each other.

Just married – with Rosemary, 1962

VIII.

Expanding My Mind

I was smart but my thinking was narrow and too conventional to be provocative or original. Dealing with my father, who would pummel me verbally if I made an argument not based on the tried-and-true, had made me cautious and not very creative. That was before I met Roger Fisher.

In my second year at Harvard Law School, while I was standing in line trying to get a drink at the black tie Christmas dinner of the law school eating club, Lincoln's Inn, a conversation nearby caught my attention. A rather tall, slender gentleman, whom I later learned was Professor Roger Fisher, was describing an article he had just written pointing out the difference between laws one should take full advantage of, like tax laws, and those like the ones against assault that one should not come close to violating. I butted in, "What about arms control laws limiting the amount of weaponry? Where do they fit in? Should we take full advantage of them and build or retain the maximum number of armaments?" Roger liked the question and turned his attention to me. We started talking about defense policy which I knew something about, and he asked me to sit next to him at dinner so that we could continue the conversation. When we finished dinner, he asked me to be his research assistant. It seemed like an interesting thing to do, and I would get paid – not much, but every bit helped since Rosemary and I were on a very tight budget.

I thought I was a fairly sophisticated thinker, particularly about arms control, after my tour in the Pentagon, but I had a lot to learn from Roger who was known for his unorthodox creative thinking, especially in the field of defense policy. He had many ideas about how we could be more effective in dealing with the Soviets - ideas which he promoted at regular intervals in Washington. When I started working with Roger, I pointed out that some of his ideas might create bad precedents. His retort startled me. "What's wrong with a bad precedent? If something doesn't work, you can change it." When people said, "We can't," Roger would say, "Why not?"

I started to do the same, particularly concerning new ideas about defense policy. My father had no interest in or knowledge about defense policy hence the subject had never come up in our frequent arguments. Never having had to take a position, I could actually look at defense issues with an open mind. Here I could be an intellectual, and Roger gave me the confidence – no, he taught me – to think for myself, to be creative. He took pleasure in my mind rather than feeling threatened by it. He didn't just teach me to think: he made discussion stimulating and conversations ceased being arguments I had to win. I was learning to listen, consider, and build on other points of view. I was taught by an intellectual ping pong champ, and it was fun to be at the table.

We worked on such legal conflicts as who owned the oil at the bottom of the Persian Gulf, Saudi Arabia or Kuwait. I don't remember which side hired Roger, but as there was no controlling law, we had to figure out how to bring the two sides together. Some of what we learned was later enshrined in Roger's book *Getting to Yes*, which is considered in many circles the negotiation bible.

I knew I needed to open my mind to issues beyond defense policy. I think Roger saw that need, and near the end of the summer in 1963 Roger unveiled a warm and original plan: Rosemary and I would come to his place in Scrubby Neck on Martha's Vineyard for a few weeks. He would engage us like an au-pair couple; we would help look after his two kids and give his wife some relief. At the same time, we were to participate in the intellectual ferment stirred by his circle of friends who were serving in the Kennedy administration and debating the issues of the day. Over beach picnics and evening cocktails we listened to Jerome Wiesner, President Kennedy's science advisor; Adam Yarmolinsky, Special Assistant to the Secretary of Defense and later poverty program maven; Kingman Brewster, Provost and soon-to-be President of Yale; and Roger toss around ideas for improving the world. We began to understand the compromises that are necessary – the countervailing arguments that have to be taken into account – to adopt well-intentioned policies. I never thought about the fact that Wiesner and Yarmolinsky were Jews in powerful government positions.

Roger was teaching me that it was okay to be an unconventional thinker, but that required my having the courage of my convictions. I'd tried that at Princeton with my senior thesis and it had almost cost me graduation. Nevertheless, in my third year in law school I took on Henry Kissinger – the foreign and defense policy guru and later Secretary of State – on the hotly debated question of the extent of the need for onsite inspection for the enforcement of arms control agreements. It wasn't quite

like taking on my father, where my psychological concerns created profound anxiety, but in my mind it was pretty big – I was
sticking my neck out. When I had challenged Admiral Burke, I
knew I was not going to stay in the Navy, but this challenge to
Kissinger could well affect my career if I ever decided to return
to the Defense Department.

I was one of 12 students in Kissinger's third-year Defense
Policy Seminar where our speakers included the Secretary of
Defense, the Chairman of the Joint Chiefs of Staff, and similar
notables. It was amazing. The major players in the design of the
country's defense had come up from Washington to talk to 12
students – because Henry asked them to.

Kissinger thought we needed unlimited onsite inspections
to be able to enforce arms control agreements. I disagreed and
wrote my third-year paper (with Roger as my advisor) laying
out my arguments with only eight footnotes, half of them from
The New York Times. This was unheard of in a law school paper
customarily laden with footnotes to support the points made.
I had only logic to support my arguments. I showed the paper
to my friend Henry Olds. He said, "It was the most frustrating
paper to read. I felt it was challenging me to disagree with your
logic, and I couldn't do it." I got an A+.

I was learning to think, but as a loner, fighting the system.
I felt good - my thinking had been vindicated – but my thumb-
in-the-eye approach was hardly diplomatic. I was more cynical
than skeptical about the established order – a carryover from
my father. As in my school days, because I did not think "they"
would treat me fairly, I believed that I could succeed only if I
went my own way.

I saw foreign policy, as Roger did, as a matter of salami
slicing, issue by issue. Yes, we opposed the Russians, but we

delivered their mail and they delivered ours, and we both adhered to the whaling treaty. We were friends with the Canadians, but we fought them tooth and nail in trade disputes and on environmental issues. I thought President Johnson should use his election campaign – which he was easily going to win over Goldwater – to educate the American people that our foreign policy was not based on absolutes - "black or white" – but on our consideration of each issue, so that he would have more flexibility in dealing with the various foreign policy issues confronting the country like Vietnam, which was raising its ugly head. Roger got me an interview with his friend Doug Cater, one of the President's Special Assistants, so that I could make that suggestion. Doug liked the idea and took it to the President. The next day he reported, "The President doesn't want to lose one vote, so the theme of the campaign is 'Don't rock the boat', but you've got a job on the President's Special Political Research Staff of six people who are to be superimposed on the Democratic National Committee for the election campaign." It was 1964. Johnson beat Goldwater in a landslide, but four years later, Johnson's presidency was destroyed because he had backed himself into a corner on Vietnam. Having made the war a moral issue, it could not be negotiated.

After I graduated, Roger continued to provide me with challenges – and they were fun. When Anguilla, a tiny Caribbean island, wanted to secede from the British Empire following a change in commonwealth arrangements that would place Anguilla under control of the dictator who ruled the neighboring island of Nevis, Roger asked me to join him in helping Anguilla to avoid this takeover. The timing was lousy – Rosemary and I were heading to Kitty Hawk, North Carolina, for a month's vacation with our month old daughter – but Roger didn't take "no" for an answer. "Just drop your wife and daughter off at Paul Warnke's house, and they can stay there until you return." I explained that we did not know Mr. Warnke, who was the U.S. arms control negotiator, and he might not appreciate the intrusion. No matter. Rosemary soon found herself changing Brooke on the Warnke kitchen table, and I took off for St. Thomas.

Roger had gathered the Anguilla cabinet in a hotel room in St. Thomas. As I entered the room, he pulled a piece of paper out of a typewriter (this was 1967 – pre-computers), announced it was a draft of the Anguillan constitution, and handed it to me with the greeting, "Jon, make it enforceable." "Sure" – I wasn't at all sure. And that was not the only problem we had to deal with in connection with Anguilla's secession. Anguilla was hardly in a good position to be on its own as a country – with one road, no telephone service and maybe a potential defense force of six policemen and four guns. However, Anguilla did not have much choice – either secede or live under a dictatorship. The "Force" must have been with us, for Roger was able to broker a deal that eventually led to Anguilla seceding from Saint Kitts and Nevis and becoming an internally self-governing overseas territory of the United Kingdom.

When I was with Roger, his intellect held sway to such an extent that it was difficult for him to deal with emotions. I remember a night when I was reading in a comfortable club chair in the living room of our New York apartment, and Roger, having just come from an interview and looking distraught, dropped on to the sofa opposite me. "Are you OK – feeling all right," I asked. He stared at me as though I had asked an impossible question. If, at this time there was flaw in his negotiating technique, it was that he did not give enough weight to the emotions of the participants. Later, in *Getting to Yes* he acknowledged that emotions had to be considered as carefully as logic, for when the negotiators are the decision makers, their emotions can often rule their thinking. (And as he became more comfortable with his emotions, he sent Rosemary and me a note with "Lots of Love, Roger.")

I later learned for myself that in a negotiation, if you let your adversary know that you understand and appreciate why he is taking a particular position, he will often go along with your solution to the conflict. That isn't being logical but is the way many people react: often feeling that being understood is more important than winning a point.

Roger was my intellectual mentor. He had a way of asking questions and thinking about issues that rubbed off on me to such an extent that when, many years later, I took my children, Brooke and Blake, to visit him, they immediately saw the resemblance: "You even talk like him," they said.

IX.

A Different Kind of Father

Sometimes you just get lucky. I certainly had my share of it from winning the NROTC scholarship, to meeting up with Jack Tomion and Squidge in the navy and being chosen by Roger as his research assistant. Fortune smiled again when I got a chance to work with Henry Harfield, one of the best and most creative lawyers I have ever met. He did for me what my own father couldn't or wouldn't. He encouraged me, challenged me, and protected me. He did not talk about it. He just did it. He became my surrogate father. If I am a good father and a good mentor, it's because Henry taught me how.

It all began on a rainy Sunday morning in Bermuda. We were on our honeymoon, and Rosemary went in search of a *New York Times* in the main house at Horizons and Cottages, an old plantation estate. Only one copy was left, and a pleasant looking young man with a rather formal manner (Troost Parker) was reading it, so she had to make friends. She did and we did. Troost, a scion of a Charlottesville, Virginia family, and Tove, an ebullient beautiful blond with Norwegian parents and an American education, were also honeymooners.

When we returned to the mainland, Troost and Tove asked

us for dinner at her parents' house in Washington. The other guest was Mike Forrestal, a fit and well-tailored 35 year-old former partner of Shearman &Sterling who was on President Kennedy's National Security Council staff. Evie and Ned Nordness, Tove's mother and stepfather, had met Mike in Norway when he and Ned were both working there on behalf of the U.S. effort in support of the Marshall Plan. Mike was then in his early 20s, having dropped out of college when his father, the first Secretary of Defense, James Forrestal, committed suicide. Ned and Evie became Mike's surrogate parents, and convinced him to go to law school.

Rosemary engaged Mike in a long conversation, and after about 25 minutes, Mike said, "I'd like to meet your husband" – a pre-feminist reaction: a smart married woman must have a smart husband. We talked for 10 minutes, and he offered me a job at Shearman & Sterling, saying his former partners would honor it. I asked, "What is Shearman & Sterling?" (One of the nation's foremost law firms, and also at that time one of the largest.) I thanked him. It was nice to have an offer in my pocket, but my focus was on government service in Washington. It would be another year before I thought about where and if I wanted to practice law. Shearman & Sterling sent me a letter honoring the offer and I never interviewed at other law firms. Mike was young, but he had influence.

Mike looked out for us in Washington and later at Shearman & Sterling. He introduced us to a world where power and elegance intersected – the world of my father's dreams. From his narrow, high-ceilinged, marbled floor office in the Executive Office Building, where most of the President's aides worked, he took us to President Kennedy's favorite Washington restaurant, Sans Souci, whose fine French cuisine attracted the powerful.

Mike's house in historic Georgetown was not particularly distinguishable from its neighbors from the outside, but inside was a world of stylish comfort and elegance. From the rich but understated furnishings to the fine art to the glass-walled dining room that opened on to a private garden, Mike's home was a bachelor's paradise. An excellent dinner cooked and served by his African-American valet was accompanied by exquisite French wine. Later as we sipped port in the library, Mike regaled us with stories about James Baldwin, the Black writer and activist, who had stayed with Mike the previous week.

Here was this man who by day talked to the President and by night lived this lush life, and he wanted to know all about us! That pumped me up and I talked freely. It never crossed my mind to mention my heritage, not because of my need to maintain the secret, but because in Washington my parents were not part of my life. In that setting I forgot about the secret and had nothing to hide. During the conversation Mike commented, "You never make any real friends after you're 25. The rest are acquaintances, relationships of convenience, not to be relied on." I suspect Mike had learned that the hard way in Washington, but what was he trying to tell us? Was he warning us not to expect too much of him? Did he want to have a way out of the relationship? Or could it be the other way round – a recognition that we might desert him? "Not a chance!" I thought. I was 26 at the time.

Several years later when Mike was back at Shearman & Sterling and Henry Harfield was in need of an associate, Mike recommended me. I wish I could say I was as good a friend to him as he had been to me, but sadly, that was not the case. Mike's warning was prophetic in a way I never could have foreseen. After I left Shearman & Sterling, too caught up in my own life, I did not keep in touch with him. It was 20 years before I reconnected, when over a three-hour lunch Mike laid out his disappointment with me. "I never heard from you. That's not the way you treat people who go out on a limb for you. You don't just cut them off." In the end, he accepted my regrets and apologies, and we agreed that he would come to dinner the following week. But it was not to be. A few days before our scheduled dinner, Mike, by then grossly overweight, but still well-tailored, died of a ruptured aneurysm. He was a good man, and I had done him wrong by failing to reach out to him. Friendship is a two-way street, and to my shame I was looking only one way. Mike's anger was justified and my remorse will haunt me forever.

Henry Harfield was the only S&S senior partner who was a generalist in the law, and he was also the lawyer to whom banking legends like Walter Wriston turned for creative solutions to difficult problems. Roger Fisher had taught me how to be creative. Henry taught me how to be practical creatively. I recall one particular example of his strategy. When he was in college at Yale and needed money, he would look in the Yale catalogue to see what prizes were available and how much each was worth. Then he found out how many students had sought each prize and applied only for those awards without competitors and picked up the money. That was vintage Henry.

With his shock of red hair and ruddy complexion, Henry always struck me as someone who was comfortable in his skin. He had not come from money and he did not like pretense. He relished telling me about the time when in grubby clothes and bare feet he greeted the immaculately dressed Chairman of Citibank who had driven out from New York to Henry's house in Westhampton to seek his advice.

I was a second year associate but Henry treated me like his partner. He told half his clients, which included most of the foreign banks with offices in New York City, to call me with any questions. "If Jon does not know the answer, he will focus the issue, and his rate is much lower than mine." Every morning he would call me into his corner office to discuss the problems he was working on. I would sit on the comfortable couch opposite his desk looking over his shoulder at the photograph of a proud Henry smiling on the deck of his boat, as he tossed out creative solutions like discs in a shooting gallery. My job was to shoot them down. The ones I missed we worked on.

Henry, a senior partner in one of the most respected law firms in the country, wanted to hear what I had to say. My own father treated me as though I was in law school. I still remember my father interrupting me at a fancy dinner as I was explaining a complex legal matter on which I was working. "Do you know what a check is," he asked – a term taught first year in law school. He had to be in control and could not accept anyone knowing what he knew – especially if that anyone was me. He could not take pleasure in what I was doing. Heck, I remember a doctor measuring my biceps and my father's during a routine examination and observing casually that mine were larger. My father snapped, "That can't be." I don't know why my father was always trying to undermine me, or why Henry was building me up.

Henry was always encouraging me to try new things in the law, which I did. I knew he would back me up if there was a glitch. I remember a client with a tax problem, which was not my field at all. Henry told me to do the research and send a memo to the head of the firm's tax department with my conclusions. I was a junior associate, and I was asking a senior partner to check my work – which was way out of the chain of command. Henry trusted me and wanted the senior people to know who I was and the kind of work I could do.

He developed my confidence, even if, sometimes, I had to call on him for help. For example, one of his foreign bank clients sent me a "term sheet" with a request that I prepare loan documents. The term sheet indicated that the loan would be secured by two types of collateral. Shortly after I got the term sheet, I called the client to ask whether they understood that the two types of collateral were interrelated in such a way that if one failed, the other failed. In effect, they only had one piece of collateral. "Oh," the client replied, "then we don't want to do the loan. Send us a bill."

I went to Henry asking how much to bill them. The whole affair had taken less than half an hour. At my then hourly rate, the bill would be less than $100. Henry told me to bill them $10,000. He said, "You've done a good job, and potentially saved them a lot of money. You've given them at least $10,000 in value." (My father would never have complimented me like that. He only told me what I did wrong.) I did what Henry said. A few days later I got a call from an irate banker asking for an explanation of the bill, since he had obviously concluded I could not have spent more than half an hour on the matter. I went back to Henry. "Tell them to pay the bill." They did. Henry made sure I got the credit when I delivered. In the same spirit of generosity, when the first litigation brief I wrote got the other side to withdraw its complaint without my having to contest it in court, Henry let me know that I had done a really good job. I wished my own father could have done the same, but it would never happen.

Henry often took me to lunch, and we regularly walked

home together. He was always interested in what I was doing and thinking. Not only did he devote himself to training me, but he also made sure the number one senior partner, Fred Eaton, knew how well I was doing – something that worked in my favor at a later date. He also arranged for me to serve on my first board of directors, The Bank of Nova Scotia Trust Company of New York, which provided me with a director's fee of $100 a meeting or $1,200 a year – meaningful when my salary at the time was $8,500. He understood how much a few extra dollars would mean. He also looked out for my professional reputation by giving me editing credit for an article he wrote for a banking journal. He always supported me when I needed it. He treated me as if I were his son.

I loved working with Henry, but a social revolution was raging in 1968, and I wanted to participate. Civil rights marches and demands for Black power, social justice, and economic opportunity were challenging the established order. President Lyndon Johnson's Great Society reforms aimed to eliminate poverty and racial injustice. In New York City, Senators Robert Kennedy and Jacob Javits had organized an ambitious effort to transform the slums of Bedford-Stuyvesant in Brooklyn, the second largest Black ghetto in the U.S., into a model community. New York's mayor, John Lindsay, had walked the streets of Harlem to avert racial violence and assure its residents that he would institute housing and other reforms they wanted and needed. The New York Urban Coalition was formed to link business leaders with leaders of the Black community and fund economic development projects that would bring jobs to Blacks and other minorities. It was an exciting time, and I wanted to be involved. In my mind a lawyer was a social architect. What was I doing in a commercial law firm when I should be doing public service, *pro bono* work. That meant leaving Shearman & Sterling, maybe never to return. I did return a year later but stayed for only 5 months.

I missed the excitement of working on policy issues that were in the press as I had in the Pentagon. I had friends who had gone to serve in Washington and others who had joined the New York City government. Rosemary was working for the Vera Institute of Justice. I was focusing on the fine print in commercial agreements, while my friends were trying to make the world a better place. I was odd man out, and I could not reconcile my private law practice with my *non sibi* Exeter training at that time of public turmoil.

With all that Henry had done for me as a father figure and a mentor, I am ashamed to say that I never took enough time to explain to him in a way he could understand why I left his tutelage to enlist in the fight for civil rights and social justice. I had wounded him. He had greatly extended himself for me, gone out on a limb for me and cleared a path to partnership in the firm. He had made a giant personal commitment and I was turning my back on him. "I just don't understand. How can you leave?" He did not deserve that. I just had to leave. I had not gone to Mississippi to support the civil rights marchers when I was in law school, but this time I had no excuse. I thought back to my days at Exeter and the school motto: *non sibi*, not for thyself. I was obligated to try to make the world a better place, but I couldn't explain it to him because I might have had to face him in an argument. I was determined to avoid the combat that was so familiar to me with my father. I just dodged the issue. It was not fair to Henry, and it was not good for me. I did not do any better when I returned to Shearman & Sterling for a few months after my year of public

service. I was assigned to a different office, and from embarrassment or self-involvement – maybe both – I did not see
Henry during that time.

What I couldn't say to Henry was that I was a Jew. "I am
not like you. You don't have any Jewish partners. I am not who
you think I am. My outward appearance and behavior is decep-
tive. My great-grandparents were killed in a pogrom. My father
had stones thrown at him because he was a Jew." I don't know
what he would have thought if I had had the courage to say
that. Pretending to be someone I wasn't had made it impossible
for me to talk freely even with my dearest friends. I couldn't be
honest with Mike Forrestal or Henry.

Twenty years after I left S&S, Henry's wife coincidentally
got out of a cab in front of our apartment house as Rosemary
was coming out the door. "Henry is still angry with Jon," she
said. He had cause, and I had the secret. We did put a band-
aid on the wound about ten years later over lunch when he
acknowledged that the firm was no longer the way it used to
be and that I had been right to leave, but our relationship was
never the same. It is my everlasting regret that I never was able
to make clear to him how important he was in my life and how
much I valued all that he did for me.

Henry had helped me develop as an independent mind. He
encouraged me to think through issues, and let me make my
own decisions. My father was too driven, anxious and frightened to permit me to find my own way. He thought his success – at least his dream –depended on my success. His attitude
towards his religion was based on the real prejudice he had
experienced, but also reflected a naïve view of the nature of
American society, and a profound ignorance of the world beyond the one in which he had grown up.

I have always been conflicted about how I should view my father. Was he a bad person? I didn't think so. He had taught me the importance of persistence and of hard work, and made me set high goals for myself. He had often been generous, but equally often used his generosity to constrain my development. His shortcomings derived from his own desire to succeed, but he had grown up without my privileges and with a tyrannical model to boot. His need to control me just as his father had tried to control him had the same disastrous effect on our relationship as it had on his own. I was not going to let that happen with my children. I would take the path Henry took with me and help them develop as independent individuals, for then there would be a chance we could have a close relationship as adults, *i.e.*, for life.

The saddest irony was this: had my father not tried to hide his Jewishness with the consequent need to control me, we would have had a different relationship and he might have been able to build on my advantages and realize his dreams of acceptance. The fact that I had been accepted meant nothing to him; perversely it seemed instead to fuel his rage and jealousy.

X.
Breaking Free

I became a father on July 28, 1967. Rosemary and I took a cab to Columbia Presbyterian Hospital that morning, and after taking pictures outside the front door to mark the occasion, we were ushered into the room where Rosemary would have induced labor – the doctor thought she was a month late. She wasn't. Several hours later, Brooke, noisy and determined, judging from the force and duration of her screaming, was born. That evening I had a question for my parents when I had dinner with them at the 21 Club, "How do you treat a girl?" "Same way as you treat a boy," my father responded. That made sense to me, but I had a much bigger problem.

How could I be a good father when my own father was still intruding on my life and always treating me like a child. Once when I offered to pay for a meal, he railed, "When you pay for a meal, I'll no longer be your father." Married and employed, I appeared to be in charge of my life, but that was not the fact. Preserving the secret that the family was Jewish tied me to him but it was slowly estranging me from my wife.

When my brother or I did something which my parents approved, they jumped to take advantage of it for themselves.

When I joined the University Club, my father's first comment was that I should get a membership card for him and my mother so that they could use the club on their own. "Not possible," I told him, "You are not members." He was disappointed and angry.

When we did something to which they objected, they raged as if we had put a stake through their hearts. At one point, Rosemary and I decided to leave St. James Church after the minister's sermon blamed loose immigration laws for the murders of Martin Luther King and Robert Kennedy. We decamped to the Madison Avenue Presbyterian Church just down the street from St. James where the minister was more to our liking. My father ranted at me on the phone for over an hour insisting that we were insulting the St. James minister whom my father had courted in his attempt to be known as an upstanding Episcopalian. What we had done was hardly unusual, but my father was sure the minister would take it as a personal affront. He didn't, but that did not calm my father.

Gifts came with strings. My father once gave a donation to a political campaign I was managing for a friend but insisted that we use it to buy radio time, which was not what we wanted the money for and not particularly helpful. When I was in high school, he said he was putting money in an account for me under the Uniform Gifts to Minors Act, which under the law would become mine outright when I was 21. But he refused to give me access to the account when I reached 21, so I needed his permission to withdraw money. The only time I succeeded with a withdrawal during his lifetime was when I threatened to go into debt if he refused to give me some of the money to take advantage of a promising investment opportunity in Baker, Weeks, a securities firm, where I was the general counsel. "You will <u>not</u> go into debt," my father declared, unable to be in debt to anyone. I remember when a broker got him to buy some municipal bonds (then considered an extremely safe investment) on margin. He didn't sleep that night and the next morning he told the broker to sell them. The Baker, Weeks investment turned out to be very profitable, by the way.

More seriously, I wondered how much longer I could keep dodging questions and lying about the secret. If I confessed, would it be better or worse for the family? Would all be forgiven? Rosemary and my younger brother, Kim, both sensed something was being hidden. At one point Kim speculated that there was a serial killer in the family and that is why he knew nothing about his relatives. The secret was badly undermining my marriage. I couldn't be honest with my wife, and withholding the truth was driving us apart. In my panic, I was critical and controlling. I kept asking Rosemary, "Do you love me?"

After 13 years of marriage, I confessed to Rosemary, "I am not who I said I was. I am a Jew." I was standing before the desk in her office cubicle at the American Bar Association where after putting her career on hold to be home with the children, she had taken a part-time position. She jumped up, threw her arms around me and said "I love you." She said, at the time, that she felt a great burden had been lifted from her shoulders now that she understood what lay behind my behavior. But the situation was more complicated. That I don't remember any of these details leads me to believe that I didn't trust her compassion. I was anxious. I could not believe all was forgiven.

And it wasn't. Our relationship had been compromised, and the bonds of trust were not so easily repaired. She had been blindsided. Neither my parents nor I looked Jewish and as far as she was aware, acted Jewish. I was a very good liar – a talented actor. She was furious with just cause. She wasn't bothered by my being Jewish. In fact, once she understood the situation, she was determined that the children would not be ashamed of being Jewish – however I felt about it. She had been toyed with – put down. I had chosen to protect my parents at her expense. Dr. Van Dusen was right: I had not separated from my parents. I had robbed her of years of conversation and intellectual interaction – all those times when I had put down her queries because I feared discovery. All this she now understood, and it would be several years and much strife before our marriage was righted.

Rosemary pressed me to tell the kids. I didn't know how to tell them. I was ashamed: there must be something wrong with me that I had to hide my identity. I delayed for several months and then told Brooke (age 8) and Blake (age 5) that I was Jewish while we were swimming or canoeing in the Berkshires, I can't remember which. They seemed to take the information aboard as a matter of small interest. In their world Jews were not subject to discrimination, and they had friends and classmates who were Jewish.

Kim was not so easy to deal with. I was ambivalent about telling him and just before I placed the call, I promised Blake we would play ball, setting up an excuse to cut the call short. However, despite Blake's pleas and my own discomfort, I could not hang up on Kim until I answered his questions: what I knew, when I knew it; what I did, why I did it?

I didn't dare tell my parents that I had revealed the secret, nor did I admit to anyone else that I was Jewish. I was afraid of the consequences: my father said he would die, my friends might cut me off. Maybe I wasn't really Jewish. I was baffled and confused. I had been baptized and confirmed as an Episcopalian my first year at Exeter, and while there, I had gone to church every Sunday. In New York, I attended St. James Church, then Madison Avenue Presbyterian, and then Holy Trinity where for a few years I was a member of the vestry.

Over the next three years Rosemary and I went to therapists – primarily to get me to understand the damage keeping the secret had done to me and to our family, and what would be necessary to heal the rifts and preserve our marriage. Finally I came around. I confronted my father and mother – in the same room in which the secret had been hatched (now the den, not my bedroom). I told them I could no longer keep the secret, and I wanted my relatives back. I waited for my father to be struck dead. My mother reacted predictably, "Now your children will not be able to get in to Harvard," she moaned. I tried to be reasonable: "Mother, more than half my class at Harvard Law School was Jewish." As usual, she missed the point and remained oblivious. My father's response was bizarre. "You are not the head of this family," he shouted. "I am the head of this family!" "You want relatives? I'll give you relatives," and he threw a cousin's wedding invitation at me.

My father did not die then – that happened a year later – but our relationship was transformed. He was no longer in charge. I had never challenged his control so directly. We continued to see each other, but our encounters often ended with his shouting at me. When we spoke on the phone, I would hold the phone away from my ear to let him fume and then I would say, "You don't mean that, Dad." It was painful. I believed he loved me even though after he died, I learned he had lied about me to my mother. He told her I had lost all my investments in Baker, Weeks, when in fact I quadrupled them, and that I was not a partner in my law firm, Christy & Viener, when I actually had been a founding partner. He also did everything he could to influence his clients not to transfer their business to me after his death. Putting all that aside, I think his anger was related more to the situation in which he found himself. He had gambled everything on his conversion, and it had not brought him happiness.

That wedding invitation he had thrown at me led me back to the family. It was an invitation from Bertram and Peg Weiss to the Westchester wedding of their daughter, Ronnie. The name Bertram Weiss did not mean anything to me, although I did remember once – I must have been about five – riding in a car sitting next to a Bobby Weiss in a naval officer's uniform.

Determined not to give up, I called Information in New Rochelle and got the number for Bertram Weiss. A man answered. "Hello. Is Bobby Weiss there," I asked. "No." Is there a Bertram Weiss there?" "Yes." "Were you ever called Bobby?" Silence. "Yes. Who is this?" I took a deep breath. "You may not remember me, but I am your cousin, Jon Masters." So ended 31 years of separation. That call led to a lunch with Bobby, now Bert, and Peg and an invitation to Ronnie's wedding.

The day of the wedding, Rosemary, Brooke, Blake and I drove to New Rochelle from the Berkshires. We had had a lovely weekend in the country, but as we got closer to New Rochelle, we started shouting at each other. We were very anxious. How would the family treat us? Would they be angry and cold because we had ignored them for so long? As we reached the synagogue entrance, we found ourselves surrounded – absolutely surrounded – by cousins, aunts, uncles – welcoming us back into the family. Bert and Peg had told everyone we were coming. Brooke and Blake met 33 relatives that day. They were overwhelmed with hugs and kisses, and their newly met cousin

Allan Kluger, who was counsel to Topps, offered to get them a complete set of that year's baseball cards – a promise on which he delivered when we visited him later in Wilkes-Barre. We could not have had a warmer welcome.

All my life my father had "threatened" me with my relatives as though their presumed inferiority would somehow pull me down. He may have been more successful financially than some of them, but on other measures like authenticity, family loyalty, and contributing to a community he was easily outclassed. Allan Kluger was head of a major law firm and a bank director. Furthermore he spent one night a week at a storefront doing pro bono legal work for whoever came in. My father could claim no such distinctions. His mark of success was that he had made more money and was the only family member to succeed – so he thought – in the wider world. Rather than staying in Pennsylvania, he had come to New York. I am glad that he did, but that hardly diminishes the lives of those who stayed. Moreover, I learned that some others did indeed come to New York and succeeded in their professions while remaining within the family and the Jewish community. They were not all heroes but they were all part of my family. I had reconnected and that felt good. No more hiding and lying.

When my father found out that I had rejoined the family, he raced back to Scranton and out to Long Island to see his brothers and sisters. If he couldn't leave them, he was going to join them – as the family leader – which is how I understood his motives. A few months later Anna, my father's oldest sister, died. When he saw me at the funeral, he said, "What are you doing here!" Now that he was part of the family, he seemed determined to shut me out, but I stood my ground. "She was my relative, too," I replied.

Since then, Rosemary and I have kept in touch with the family, participated in reunions, visited cousins, regularly spent Passover with Bert's sister, and had dinners with Bert and Peg. But if rejoining the family was one thing, returning to the Jewish fold was something else. I was a Jew because I had been born to Jewish parents, not because I practiced the religion. Passover was a family gathering rather than a religious occasion. The only religious services I had attended for most of my life were Christian. There was one way, however, in which I was culturally Jewish: I truly valued intelligence.

I did not want to be an adherent to any organized religion. My experience with anti-Semitism and anti-Catholicism had taught me that joining one religion meant demonizing others. Religions were exclusionary and that was not for me. It wasn't that I didn't believe in God. I had prayed to God every night of my life. But being religious to me was about having values, caring about people. When I told funny stories about Moses and Aaron, I was not making fun of the Jewish Exodus from Egypt. I was making a more general point about slavery and tyranny.

The reunion with the family did not have the same effect on my brother. Kim was my parents' conversion success story. Raised to believe he was an Episcopalian, his religion was important to him. The family album had pictures of Kim as a choir boy. He was unpleasantly shocked to receive the news that he was a Jew but that was not unexpected. He had grown up not knowing his anxious and demanding parents were Jews trying to fit into a Christian community and that he had Jewish relatives. I had grown up knowing I had relatives, and with parents who knew who those relatives were. I could make some sense of the way our parents acted. He could not. Our levels of self-confidence reflected that difference. My connecting with our

Jewish family was not something to which he could easily or willingly relate.

Over time, I gradually became more comfortable with my identity and told friends I was a Jew. This led to my being more open, more willing to share experiences, more confident and less fearful of close relationships. It has made me a kinder person, more able to empathize and be helpful to others who face difficult issues.

XI.

Being a Father

I wanted very much to be a good father, and given Brooke's expectations, the bar was set pretty high. On Fathers' Day when she was eight years old, she gave me the following letter. The framed original sits on my desk.

Dear Dad

I guess being a father isn't easy
It would probably make me queasy
But you aren't just one in a crowd
Youre my father which makes me proud

If Im in trouble and I need help
Youre always there before I let out a yelp
If I ever need a sholder to cry on
Youll be there even during a cyclon(e)

Dads are something no one else can be
Not a grandfather or even a mommy
Im writing this message just for to say
Youre a great dad have a great Fathers Day

Your loving Brooke

Like many parents, I suspect, I wanted to do for my children what had not been done for me. I had always felt like an outsider. Always out of place, I had no community to which I could naturally turn. I did not want my children to be in that situation.

I wanted them to feel loved and respected, listened to, and praised when that was appropriate. Far from controlling them, I wanted them to be independent. If they could stand on their own, I believed we would we be able to stand together when they were adults. That was the lifelong relationship I wanted to have with my children.

Rosemary shared these goals. Whatever our differences, when it came to the children, we spoke with one voice. Their needs came first. I think they knew that from an early age, for whenever as toddlers they had the croup in the middle of the night, Rosemary and I would be with them in the bathroom with the shower running. We took turns. She would sing to them, I would tell them about Tugboat Annie, stories they still remember. Breakfasts, dinners, and weekends were family time.

A loner for most of my life, I did not naturally gravitate to a community, much as I wanted to be part of one whose values I shared and would accept me for who I was. A church or synagogue was out, given my experience with religion. I wanted the community to be based someplace where we could relax together as a family and have friends, which meant it would have to be away from our high-pressure jobs and thus outside the city. I wanted a family-oriented place. By chance, a year before Brooke was born we found it.

That spring and summer I had managed the political campaign for the Democratic Congressional nomination of Peter Berle, a friend and law school classmate. To thank me, Peter's parents invited us to their house in the Berkshires for Labor Day weekend. That led to their "renting" us the house, "Hillside", across the road from them for $100 for our summer vacation month. Brooke celebrated her first birthday at Hillside with the Berles and the Carswells who were related by marriage. As soon as we could afford our own house, the Berkshires became our weekend refuge.

I think Brooke and Blake thought of the Berkshires as home more than New York City. Friday evenings we would pull down the backseat in our yellowish green 1972 Toyota Corona Mark II station wagon (known as "Grass"), lay out sleeping bags for the kids, and head off to our house in Mill River. Today, we would be arrested for endangering our kids. On the way, we sang (me off key) and told Exodus stories, which I embellished – transforming Moses into a golfer hitting his ball into the burning bush while Aaron became a lawyer presenting the case for liberation to the Pharaoh.

Rosemary and I never took our work with us. We had no television in the Berkshires. We entertained ourselves. Imaginative play was the order of the day. Brooke often complained that she had to make up all the games because Blake had no imagination. Today Blake lives by his imagination as a screenwriter, and Brooke, a reporter, deals with facts. Entertainment was attending outdoor performances of Shakespeare at the

Our family – reading to Brooke and Blake, c. 1972

Mount, Edith Wharton's Berkshire home, and enjoying a picnic there. Sometimes we fell asleep during the play; more often, Shakespeare triumphed.

We did things as a family, and we spent time with other families, especially the Berles, Carswells and Prisendorfs (a New York family who had moved to the Berkshires and ran the local newspaper, *The Berkshire Record*), all of whom had children the ages of Brooke and Blake and all of whom remain friends to this day. There were no cocktail parties. Families would visit families.

We all grew up together developing yearly traditions like the Pinnacle climb the Sunday before Labor Day. We shared drinks and deviled eggs at the foot of Pinnacle mountain on our friend Angie Wagner's property before climbing to the top for a bring-or-cook-your-own picnic. Rosemary describes Blake's first climb and other events in an account she wrote for the 40th anniversary of the Pinnacle climb.

Memories of Pinnacle
1972-2012

Blake's first climb

Blake, not yet three had heard all about the steep, challenging climb to the Pinnacle summit from his big sister, Brooke, and her friends. He was determined to make the climb on his own. His Dad offered to carry him, "No, Daddy, I will do it myself." We followed his chubby little legs, step by determined step to the top, over rocks, sliding in steep places, until at last he reached the glorious view at the top. He was as proud as Edmund Hillary at the peak of Mount Everest.

Marshmallows

Each year the contest: Who could make the most perfectly roasted marshmallow? Year in and year out (or so it seemed), Kate Carswell won the prize, with the golden gleaming, all around, perfectly gooey inside marshmallow without a single leak. Ten years later, Kate became one of Pinnacle's official marshmallow judges. Remembering tears of contests past, she awarded prizes for the ugliest, the best tasting, the most unusual and a few other categories so that in the end no one felt left out.

Northern Lights

On just one climb as the darkness came on, Angie called out, "Look, everyone! It's the northern lights!" And sure enough the northern sky shimmered with an immense curtain of green, blue and an occasional shaft of red. It was a magical night, this sight so seldom seen in Pinnacle's latitude. We watched in awe and felt at one with the universe.

The Environmentally Correct Lion Hunt

The culmination of each Pinnacle climb was Peter Berle reciting to wide eyed children the call and response of the old children's game of the Lion Hunt. "Do you want to go on a lion hunt?" he would boom out in his wonderful deep voice. "OK let's go." "OK, let's go," the kids (and most adults) would call back. Off he would take them, through the grass, across the bridge, through the mud, up the tree, down the tree, up the cliff and into the cave where he and they would encounter a warm breath, long whiskers and sharp teeth. "It's a lion!" Peter would shout. "It's a lion!" we would shout back. Off we would go, all pell-mell back through the identical steps, until out of breath we were all home safe. We all learned the power of imagination then, because, even though we knew it was a game, our hearts would be beating fast, and our legs trembling just a bit.

As years went by, Peter introduced into the game a little propaganda which expressed his dedicated commitment to saving the environment. Cameras, not guns would be put into our backpacks. Stones displaced from the trail would be replaced and tossed soda cans picked up (both going and coming), endangered species would be identified and celebrated. Finally, when the time came and Peter could no longer make the climb, that sweet determined little boy who had made the climb on his little chubby legs, now grown to manhood with his own big, booming voice, led the Lion Hunt himself in honor of his godfather, Peter.

What It All Means

For forty years as the sun began to move south, we celebrated the end of summer on Pinnacle Peak. We celebrated the unending cycle of light, darkness and the renewal of light. We celebrated also the cycle of life. Strong adults became old, but small children became strong, competent adults with children of their own.

How blessed we all are, we who have made the climb at Pinnacle. Blessed in friends, and family and the unimaginable beauty of this earth and this life.

The tradition continues. We are now in our third Berkshire house with accommodations for the whole family and a 30-mile view to the west. The grandkids come for visits, and the property has been put in trust so that hopefully it will pass to Brooke and Blake in a manner that will allow them to retain it for future generations. After being on the outside for so long, it feels very good to be a member of this community and even better to know that my children are.

I also wanted them to have confidence in their own abilities, to know that they can succeed at whatever they choose if they are willing to work and persevere. We sent them to good schools where they got individual attention. When Brooke's class at Brearley was asked to write stories, her motor skills had not developed sufficiently for her to write clearly. Instead of forcing her to write, the teacher had Brooke dictate her stories until her motor skills improved. Today Brooke is a professional writer. I doubt that would be the case had she been forced to write before she was able. Blake had early dyslexia. He knew that "cat" had three letters, a "c", "a" and "t", but he could not get the order straight. The teachers at Town school realized that Blake was very bright but needed help to overcome this problem. They gave him special tutoring until he got his dyslexia under control. He, too, is now a successful writer. "Spell check" and computers help, but that early experience taught him how he could overcome his limitations with hard work and perseverance.

We encouraged them to think for themselves and take charge of their lives. When Brooke was in fourth grade we attended a parents' meeting where the biggest concern was how they could know what homework was being assigned. Rosemary and I looked at each other. We had never even thought about getting involved with homework. As Blake later remarked, homework was his and Brooke's job, and "like any job, we are expected to do it well." I believe he got that expectation from us although I am pretty sure we had never said it precisely, but the pressure must have been there. Of course, Rosemary and I were available for questions, but homework was their business.

Dinners in the City were also family affairs. After Rosemary returned to full-time work, dinners were at eight o'clock. That meant that while we had hired someone to be at home and greet the children when they returned from school, Brooke and Blake would do their homework and get their baths on their own. Having a late dinner was not great, but it was the earliest we could all eat together. And having dinner together was important. (In fact, in the year Brooke graduated from high school, a survey of National Merit Scholars determined that the characteristic most had in common was that they had dinner with their parents.)

Blake pointed out that we ate in 15 minutes and talked for an hour and three-quarters. We talked about our lives, at work, at school, the issues of the day, politics, international affairs, law, justice, ethical behavior – whatever. When Bernie Goetz shot four young men who tried to rob him on a subway train, it was a hot topic for us for weeks as we argued about the appropriateness of his conviction. We argued and often disagreed. As Blake said, "In our family, argument is sport." That was pretty hard on Blake because he was three years younger than Brooke whose verbal skills were extraordinary. But as he told us at the time, "When I look at the second children of your friends, I see I have a choice. I can rebel or compete. I'll compete." And compete, he did - in his own way. Rosemary, Brooke and I would be talking about some issue, and Blake would make a comment that seemed to be totally unrelated to our discussion. About a minute later, it would dawn on us that he had seen the issue from a totally different perspective which we had missed.

Sometimes, however, arguments got out of hand. Rosemary, a student of John Milton's literary style, described the Gettysburg Address as an excellent example of Miltonian prose. I countered that Lincoln's language was repetitious. Brooke took my side. The argument became personal: I wasn't an intellectual, and I didn't appreciate literary tradition. We were having dinner in the Berkshires. Blake had had enough. He got up from the table, got his bicycle and rode around the living room and dining area until we stopped. By the way, Rosemary was absolutely right about the Gettysburg Address, as I had to concede when I read it aloud at the Memorial Day service in Mill River, Massachusetts.

The problem was mine. While I would listen to Rosemary, Brooke and Blake, I was often too quick to try to impose my own view. I had never engaged in discussions growing up – and certainly not about intellectual topics. Conversation with my parents involved either lectures or arguments. If I hadn't fought back against my father, I would have been run over. Discussions were contests to win or lose which drove Rosemary up a wall. She had grown up in an environment that cherished intellectual discussion: everyone learned and ideas were piled one on another. It took me a long time to break my old habit, but now I think I am a pretty good – though not perfect – listener and collaborator

Brooke and Blake warned their friends to be prepared if they came to dinner, they could be asked about anything. Those dinner conversations gave Brooke and Blake a sense of confidence – a willingness to speak out even when they knew others would challenge them. No doubt that helped them when they went to Exeter and engaged in discussions around the Harkness table where students and teacher learned through debate. Academics were never an issue in our household. Brooke and Blake were always good students, and while we did not want to pressure our children to succeed, somehow that message got through, although I also think they had a certain pride in doing well.

Contrasted with the pressures of their Manhattan elementary schools with their high-performing, highly competitive students, weekends in the Berkshires were therapeutic. Bob Fleury who lived next door to us was a brilliant unlicensed architect who had escaped from New York City in the 1960s to live in the Berkshires. With very little money, his children, Tais and Jared, depended for much of their entertainment on highly developed imaginations. Together with Brooke and Blake they created an imaginary sports complex, a real baseball team, played *Star Wars* games and built the sets to go with them. Rosemary and I loved watching and listening.

We wanted Brooke and Blake to learn about life beyond the schoolroom. We wanted them to be comfortable with highly accomplished people and at the same time to know that even those people "put their pants on one leg at a time." Our friends in the Berkshires made the point for us. The fathers Brooke and Blake saw in jeans and work-boots driving tractors, digging post-holes, almost losing a toe trying to kill a raccoon with an axe, doing chores and dealing with family issues were the same people who in their day jobs were prominent government officials, successful politicians, and leaders of major law firms, huge financial institutions and other major organizations.

We were regulars at museums and Broadway shows and went to whatever cultural events we thought might interest Brooke and Blake. Although the ups and downs of my legal income often made it touch and go, we traveled a fair amount as a family - usually during spring vacation but sometimes in the summer or at Christmastime. Apart from several skiing trips to

Alta, Utah, and a week in Hawaii, most of our travel was to the Caribbean or Europe. When they were 13, each child got to go with one parent anywhere in the world they wanted for three weeks. The only requirement was that they had to plan the trip. Brooke went with Rosemary to Great Britain. Blake and I went to Greece and Crete.

Our children were our priority. Rosemary left her high-powered job to be home with them during their early years. I always felt that being a father was the most important responsibility I had. We listened to them, but we did not try to take over their lives. I remember when Brooke asked which elective she should take in her second year in high school, I asked her to list the pros and cons for each. When she finished with the pros and cons, I told her that she now had all the facts she needed to make her decision. Even today when they ask for my advice, I focus on helping them identify and weigh the consequences of their options rather than on making the final decision which should be theirs.

We tried to do our best. We loved them. Blake gave me this report card on my 60th birthday:

> ## MY FATHER'S REPORT CARD
> *My father can't dance though he likes to snap his*
> *fingers and bounce out of time to Tom Paxton.*
> *A for effort. D for execution.*
>
> *My father is mechanically inept but he still taught me*
> *how to use a chainsaw. Somehow we both still have*
> *all our fingers.*
> *A for effort. C for execution.*

*My father let me drive his Porsche, let me drink in
the house, let me do Richard Pryor routines at the
table, taught me how to make a martini.
A for effort. Lowered to A- (he sold the Porsche).*

*My father taught me to carve, let me win at gin,
still pays for golf, taught me to sing the wrong
words to "We Three Kings", taught me Moses was
a golfer and Aaron was a lawyer.
All A's.*

*My father was always home for dinner: A
My father always takes my calls: A*

*I have never doubted, even for a moment that my
father loves me with all his heart: A+*

—————— XII. ——————

Figuring Out My Priorities

Even as I was struggling to keep the family secret, I was re-
pressing it in pursuit of my dream of becoming Secretary of State.
That was my ambition as I told Rosemary before one of our first
dates. Now that I was no longer constrained by the secret, I did
not have to live a split life or hide my heritage. It was never a
matter of being a Jew. Kissinger was Secretary of State and no
one suspected him of being a WASP. It was my fear of being in
the spotlight exposing my lies and harming my parents. Now I
could be in the limelight. Was that still what I wanted?

I was 40 years old looking back at where I had been to figure
out where I wanted to go. I realized how much, in my early
20's, I had enjoyed working on national security issues in the
Pentagon on the staffs of the Chief of Naval Operations, the
Under Secretary of the Army and the Assistant Secretary of
Defense for International Security Affairs. I had had a role –
admittedly very minor - in developing national security policy,
and issues on which I had been involved were hot topics in the
press. I felt I was somebody – not a potential social outcast.

I had always liked politics – essential if you want a political appointment. I had been a political junkie ever since the

1960 West Virginia Democratic primary when Kennedy beat Humphrey in the run up to that year's national convention to select a presidential candidate. I had attended that national convention in Los Angeles with an English friend I had met at a party in Georgetown on my 23rd birthday. We managed to wangle introductions to both John Connally of Texas and Lyndon Johnson's key backer, and Carmine DeSapio, Boss of Tammany Hall, of whom Ed Koch, later New York's mayor and a former rival, reputedly said, "He's a crook, but I like him." Connally glad-handed us and gave us two passes to attend the convention for a day. DeSapio, behind his dark glasses was not effusive. "Hello. Nice to meet you. What do you want?" I was learning: there are different types of politicians – the glad-hand-er who runs for office and the wary political boss.

After that first day, when passes got us through the gates, we had to sneak in: One day I got in by carrying flowers to Lyndon Johnson. On other days I may simply have gone behind a guard's back or through an unattended door. I was accomplished at such maneuvers because, as a teenager, I had crashed a number of hotel dances in New York by going through the kitchen. At any rate, we were on the convention floor with the delegates to see and hear John Kennedy get the nomination on the first ballot. Heady stuff for a kid.

Four years later at 27, thanks to Roger Fisher's recommendation, I attended the Democratic National Convention in Atlantic City, New Jersey, as a member of Lyndon Johnson's political research staff where I had been doing opposition research and writing statements which would be handed out at Republican rallies undercutting the speaker's support of Senator Barry Goldwater. Looking down from my glassed-in office far above the convention floor of Boardwalk Hall, with the delegates waving placards for their candidates and their states, I could hear Senators and Congressmen say what campaign strategists had told me to tell them to say. They never refused. Crossing Johnson was too risky. I also learned that just because a politician says something, it doesn't mean he believes it or will act on it.

Two years later in 1966 I got to run my first campaign - as the manager for my friend and law school classmate, Peter Berle, a ruggedly handsome former paratrooper whose father had been a prominent liberal member of President Franklin Roosevelt's "kitchen cabinet". Barely out of law school, we tried to overthrow the establishment candidate and win the Democratic Congressional nomination for New York City's Silk Stocking District, the upper east side of Manhattan. I had convinced Peter that, despite his desire to be in control of his life, he could not run his own campaign. "You are out front," I told him, "You can't see what else is going on." At first reluctantly, and then wholeheartedly as his confidence grew, he put me in charge of the campaign. It was great: I made the backroom decisions but wasn't in the limelight – the family secret was back in my consciousness with my family nearby and anti-Semitism still an issue with some people I had to deal with. Being out of the limelight was the compromise. It was fun being in charge and challenging the establishment. Peter walked every block of the district and his handshake was so strong that when voters saw him coming, they often shied away: "I'll vote for you, but please don't shake my hand," they would say with a smile. We got 400 volunteers, mostly young lawyers, to help us. Valiant try, but we lost that time. Later in 1968, 1970, and 1972, we helped Peter win election to the New York Assembly three times.

At Shearman & Sterling, I was seen as someone who eventually would be going back and forth to government service. But that was all in the future and I couldn't wait. It was 1968 - the country was in turmoil; my friends and I were protesting against the Vietnam War, advocating for civil rights, supporting the War on Poverty, and urging the passage of the Fair Housing Act. We were on the sidelines cheering. I wanted to do more. As someone who had been the subject of discrimination as a child, I hated injustice. I was skeptical of authority and protective of vulnerable people. Full time public service was calling.

I said as much at dinner one night to an S&S partner, Myles Whalen, who relayed my thoughts to the Senior Partner, Fred Eaton. The next morning on my desk was a note. "See me, Fred Eaton." I did, of course. Fred Eaton dressed like the senior managing partner he was with stiff white collars mounted on colored shirts with initialed French cuffs. A man to be taken seriously, he was very pleasant and very direct. I went into his paneled office after passing through his secretary's outer office and was greeted with a surprise: "What's this, I hear you want to leave?" I was taken aback. "I want to do public service," I said. He didn't miss a beat: "You want to work for John Doar?" (John Doar, formerly Kennedy's Assistant Attorney General for Civil Rights, had requested help for a project to transform the Bedford-Stuyvesant section of Brooklyn, which had become the second largest ghetto in the United States.) "We don't want to lose you," he continued. Henry Harfield and Mike Forrestal had sold me to Fred Eaton so well that after only three years, it was a given that I would be a partner. "If you want to work for John Doar," he said, "we will continue to pay you and you will maintain your seniority." (Eaton was so generous, I felt a bit sheepish, because in my days with the Navy, I had helped to shoot down an arms control proposal that he, as the U.S. Arms Control negotiator, had submitted for approval. He did not know this, and I did not bring it to his attention.)

My job for the Bedford-Stuyvesant D&S Corporation was to go to Washington, discover which departments controlled the funds for the project and figure out how to get them. I learned my way around several government departments and wrote what became the road map for funding the rebirth of Bed-Stuy as a commercial hub and a safe and affordable community. The work was interesting and challenging, but I wanted to do more than sit around my office – actually a former bedroom in the rundown Grenada Hotel, 4 bare walls, 2 desks and 4 chairs – waiting for John Doar to give me another assignment. John, tall, thin and imposing, always looked relaxed but in fact was an intense, energetic leader determined to get his way. It was said that left alone, he did the work of 10 people. But he did not get much more work done with a large staff. Demanding complete control, he personally approved every assignment. Individual initiative was not just discouraged, it was banned. Unwittingly, I had gone to work for a man who in some ways was like my father.

My officemate and I had many ideas about how to do more for the Bed-Stuy community, but we could not get John to focus on them. We got frustrated, and like the inexperienced bureaucrats we were, we did something really stupid. We formed Creative Action Corporation with a professor who was an expert in early childhood development and used our office secretary to type a request for a federal grant. We did not think of ourselves as competing with the Bedford-Stuyvesant D&S Corporation for federal money because that organization had no plans to be active in early childhood development. However, we did use the corporation's resource – our secretary – to type our proposal. John, like many intensely driven leaders, valued loyalty above everything. He called us in to his hotel room office – decorated only with books and papers on the floor – shook his head, and in a calm but firm voice dismissed us, "I can't have you around here. You can resign or I'll fire you." In his mind, by organizing Creative Action Corporation, planning to apply for federal funds, and using our secretary to type the proposal, we had been disloyal to the corporation. We resigned.

John had a point. Our frustration had blinded us to the implications of what we were doing. Furthermore, if we had gone to him – not behind his back – with our proposal, he might have allowed us to take it forward under the auspices of the Bedford-Stuyvesant D&S Corporation, and we would have accomplished what we wanted. Many of my reactions to authority had been influenced by my father. I would have ignored my father, and I had chosen to ignore John in the same way. I will never be sure if that was the only reason I didn't go to John first. Rosemary had warned me that we would get fired. But I went ahead anyway. On the other hand, I did exactly what my father would have done, "Pay no attention to the rules. You can get away with it." The established order was not to be trusted. Prosper in spite of the system - the premise of the secret. I was a living paradox, ignoring my father but acting like him.

As I looked back, I realized my Bedford-Stuyvesant experience was a wake-up call. I did not think I was unethical, but I had not given any consideration to the ethics of what I was doing. I was just barreling ahead. I had to stop and rethink. Maybe the rules were not all bad, not all out to get me. Maybe there was a time to stand on line. What did I believe? What were my ethics? How did I want to live my life? I did not want to give up on public service, but my *modus operandi* would have to change.

I was also learning that public service work had its problems. My heart may have been in the right place, but there were limits to what could be done. A senior government official told me that if he always voiced his opinion about what he thought was best, he would alienate others and get nothing done. He had to choose one or at most, two issues on which he would try to make progress and give in on the rest. Not ideal, but practical. Moreover, to advance to positions of leadership, one had to spend a huge amount of time – away from family – on mind-numbing activities like meet-and-greet functions and endless committee meetings on inconsequential subjects. Not glamorous, but necessary.

I wasn't completely put off, but it was clear that if I was going to enter public service, I needed money. Money had derailed Peter Berle's political career when he proved unwilling to raise the large sums needed for election. (He gave up politics to become a leading environmentalist – and Blake's godfather.) Another friend's family found their budget very tight when he served as Deputy Secretary of the Treasury. Where could I get enough money to afford to enter public service and still take care of my family - with two children in private schools and two mortgages?

My first thought was to return to Shearman & Sterling and try to become one of the partners who went back and forth to government and earned a lot of money in the interim practicing law. On reflection, however, that prospect did not seem attractive. My peers were not likely to look kindly on me: "The only thing you are in training for is senior partner." A criticism, not a joke. Senior partner would not be bad, but given my brash, outspoken manner, I would never be elected by my colleagues.

More likely to me was the probability of some sort of repeat of my St. Bernard's experience – defeat and ostracization. Nor did I want to be like my peers - working long hours on projects that did not interest me. There may also have been another reason for my reluctance to cast my lot with Shearman & Sterling: a hidden but very real fear of how they would react if they were to find out I was a Jew. As far as I knew, S&S had never had Jewish partners.

Nonetheless in the summer of 1969, after my colossal Bedford-Stuyvesant mistake, I did go back to Shearman & Sterling. I needed a job. Fortunately, John never told S&S about what I had done and Fred Eaton welcomed me with open arms, although he was not happy when I said, "I'm not sure I want to be a partner." I wanted a part-time job, I told him, so that I could figure out what I wanted. I think he thought I was crazy, but apparently he recognized something in me that I did not see. "OK, but we're paying you full-time," he replied. "I never want it known that anyone at Shearman & Sterling works part-time." This was an immensely kind offer – probably unlikely today.

In the end, I concluded Shearman & Sterling was not the right place for me long-term. I had learned at an early age to listen to my own voice. Because I had always been on my own, it was easier for me to make decisions without concern for the opinions of others – for better or worse. When I told my father that I intended to leave S&S, he went ballistic. "How can you be so stupid! You would have everything. You would be accepted everywhere," he shouted, oblivious to the patrons surrounding us in the very modern elegant outer dining room of the Four Seasons restaurant. How could I turn down an almost certain Shearman & Sterling partnership – an opportunity he would have loved to have had? I explained that the trade-offs (occasional government appointments and high pay vs. long hours away from my family, the frustrations of bureaucracy and peer envy - isolating me again) were, to my mind, not worth it. It was useless: He could not understand. He scoffed at me for turning away and would never admit to me or himself how his own torturous path had created awful problems for his sons.

Even before I revealed the secret, I had started thinking about how I might work on public policy issues without making the necessary financial sacrifices. I needed to make money if I wanted, as I did, to send my children to the" best" schools. A securities firm client, Baker, Weeks & Co, Inc., with whom I had been working, asked me to be their general counsel and their face to regulators and Washington. Wall Street was on the brink of change: institutions were replacing individuals as the dominant shareholders, and they wanted cheaper commissions (negotiated commissions rather traditional fixed rates) and the ability to do their own trades without having to use a broker. When I realized that the structure of the securities industry would have to change to accommodate the demands of the institutions, I jumped at the opportunity. Baker, Weeks was probably the most respected institutional research firm in the country, and their opinion on the restructuring would undoubtedly be sought by both regulators and legislators. I could have an effect on public policy, and I did, serving on an advisory committee to the Securities and Exchange Commission and various other industry committees. My greatest influence was helping draft the 1975 Securities Acts Amendments protecting payments for research and providing market access for institutions.

The research that brokerage firms provided investors on securities was paid for by the high fixed commission rates. The fear was that negotiated commission rates would mean the end of securities research if institutions could not pay more than the lowest commission rates without violating their fiduciary duties to their clients. Working with Harvey Pitt, then Executive Assistant to the Chairman of the Securities and Exchange Commission, over a take-out Chinese dinner at his house, we drafted the provision, which became law, allowing fiduciaries to pay up for research. On institutional access, I was at the "table" when the legislation was being drafted. (Worried both about the effect on the securities markets and banks taking too much risk, I had urged that the Glass-Steagall Act restrictions on affiliations between commercial banks and securities firms not be loosened any further.) At the time, Baker, Weeks seemed to offer the perfect solution: I was influencing policy but remaining mostly out of sight.

As satisfying as that was, the more I saw how things worked, the more I began to have second thoughts about government service. An aide to Senator Pete Williams, the chairman of the Senate Securities Subcommittee, asked our firm to testify at the Subcommittee hearing to support the proposed legislation. When I called him to accept, he said he wanted us to make a contribution to Senator Williams campaign. Something did not smell right. I did not like connecting the contribution to the testimony. We did not contribute – or testify. Whether connected or not, a few years later Senator Williams was convicted for taking bribes in the Abscam scandal. Politics I had come to see had plenty of its own secrets.

My job in the private sector, at Baker, Weeks, where I worked from 1969 to 1976, age 32 to 39, was fun – and fulfilling. I was given my head, and I flourished. It was an old fashioned company where ethical lapses were not tolerated and good work was rewarded. In addition to opportunities to shape securities regulation and legislation and participate in industry councils, I traveled to interesting places all over the world to further the firm's business and deal with challenging issues. I was having a good time, earning a good living, and spending time with my family.

Was public service still my priority? I wanted to do good, but I had learned that public service was not all about doing the right thing. My Baker, Weeks experience taught me that I could contribute from the private sector without having to make the compromises required of those in government or politics. I could also make more money than I could as a government employee. Most important, I loved my children and my wife, and I was determined to help them overcome the family trauma and realize their potential. I couldn't do that and make the time commitment required by public service. If there was a defining moment, it was when I went to the airport with a lawyer friend to meet our daughters who were coming back from a trip abroad. My friend had been traveling extensively, leaving home for weeks at a time, as he devoted his life to public service. When the girls walked off the plane, my friend and his daughter shook hands. That said worlds to me about their relationship. I knew it was not for me. Brooke and I hugged and kissed. I didn't want to be the distant father I would be if I were to devote myself to public service. I didn't want my children longing, as I had, for a father they could turn to for companionship and support. I wanted to be the father I didn't have, and my public service career would have to adapt to that priority rather than the other way around. At 40 I knew that for me what really mattered was family.

With Rosemary on my 40th birthday, 1977.

XIII.

Realizing My Priorities

Given the turmoil created by my struggle to keep the secret, my focus on my wife and children was a wise decision. But what did it mean for my work life to put family first? I needed a good income to send my children to private schools as I had been sent and because Rosemary wanted to change careers and needed additional schooling and professional training. While I did not want money to control my life, I did want interesting and challenging work. "How could you pass up Shearman & Sterling" was a refrain I heard from some of my old law school classmates – and, of course, from my father. I wondered whether they thought I was lazy, that I did not want to work as hard as S&S lawyers did – and as they did in their respective firms. That was their choice, but why should it define *my* life? I was desperate to heal the wounds caused by my secrecy and I both needed and wanted to spend more time with my family. I was going to take charge of my life – I felt I was entitled to do that.

Just because I put my family first did not mean that I did not want to have a successful career. Like my father I was ambitious and like him I wanted to do well on my own terms. I wanted to work with interesting, bright colleagues who cared about each other and had high ethical standards. Baker,Weeks was no longer the answer. Even with the favorable legislation protecting research firms, it would be very difficult for Baker, Weeks to survive for long as an independent entity. When I left Baker, Weeks in 1976 after seven years, the Chairman, Charlie Mott, with whom I had worked closely and enjoyably, asked me to remain as their general counsel and as a director. That meant I had a sizable client, which in turn meant that I needed to join a law firm which could deliver a variety of services.

Reaching out in every way I could, I finally connected with someone on the law school grapevine who told me that one of my Harvard classmates, John Viener, was planning to start a law firm with Arthur Christy, a former U.S. Attorney for the Southern District and a friend of Henry Harfield. I called John, whom I remembered as a smart, polished, driven student with a gracious Southern manner – he was from Richmond, Virginia – and we met in the library of his antique-filled apartment. After I explained my situation, though not the fact I had been born a Jew, John thought I would be a welcome addition to the group – especially since I had Baker, Weeks as a client. The decision, however, was not his alone. I would have to talk to each of the other prospective founding partners. I liked that – everyone had a say.

After meeting with each of them, I was invited to join the group of founding partners, even though I made clear that my family – not the firm – would be my first priority. If that meant I got less money, so be it. The six of us formed a law firm, Christy & Viener, which turned out to be an extraordinary collaboration, especially for the first ten years - before we took on a significant number of partners from the outside. We cared about each other and wanted our partners to succeed in ways of their own choosing. We did not have a managing partner and made decisions together. We were five assimilated Jews and one Christian with similar educational backgrounds – two colleges (Princeton and Yale) and two law schools (Harvard and Columbia). I felt comfortable with this group and though it was not a conscious thought, I must have sensed that if I acknowledged my Jewish heritage – which I did in 1977, the year after we formed the firm – I would not be a social outcast. My confidence was not misplaced. What was a pivotal event in my life was a non-event to my partners. The biggest reaction was "Oh, that's interesting." They accepted me just as they had before I told them the secret.

Christy & Viener, with its camaraderie and eccentricities, was the mirror image of a family. Instead of going to the office during the 1977 citywide power outage to make the most of the daylight, we spent the day with our wives having fun at a partner's old farmhouse and his swimming club. Every year we had a party where everyone who worked in the firm – not just lawyers – brought their families to watch the Christmas tree lighting at Rockefeller Center from our office in the British Empire building in the complex. Arthur Christy dressed as Santa gave gifts to all the children, as Brooke, Blake – and as many others who would fit – sat on the window sills in my large office watching the show through two big windows facing the skating rink. When one of our young associates was dying of AIDs, we kept him on the payroll, offered him opportunities to do meaningful work when he was able, and adjusted our insurance to cover his medical needs. Many years later when the firm was no more, two of the young lawyers whom the firm had nourished told me, "Christy & Viener will always be our home. Our current firm is just a job."

We respected one another and accepted our differences. I could be who I wanted to be. We allowed each other that freedom, in stark contrast to the pressure my parents had put on me to conform to their imager of what was appropriate. The three offices that overlooked the skating rink – Arthur's, John's, and mine – sent very different messages. Arthur's was very functional like the litigator he was, both worldly, with a large map of the globe on one wall, and determined, with a picture on another wall of himself in climbing gear hanging from a high wire crossing a canyon on an Outward Bound trip. John's office was traditional, full of antiques, comforting and familiar to wealthy clients. In my office – not afraid to let people see that I was different – I let myself go: a pair of burnt red suede designer chairs with burnished metal arms faced a large Brazilian rosewood desk I had designed behind which was my tall dark brown leather desk chair. Opposite the desk were two matching club chairs and a large soft welcoming couch – long enough for me to stretch out on. On the wall behind my desk – to give clients a touch of informality - was a joyful painting of a surfboarder riding close to the leading edge of a wave. The wall opposite my desk held a large tumultuous abstract painting to remind me of the turmoil that brought my clients to my office and on which I needed to focus. Looking back, I think both the surfboarder and the abstract reflected the tensions in my life.

Because my personal idiosyncrasies were tolerated I found myself thinking more and more about the kinds of things that gave me pleasure, and that I had almost forgotten in my determination to make money. I had always loved acting, but had sublimated my feelings about the theatre as I pursued my legal career. At Christy & Viener, determined to test my abilities, I enrolled in acting classes. On Thursday afternoons I closed my office door, changed into a sweatshirt and jeans, walked past the secretaries to the elevator, and headed off to acting class where I crawled on the floor with 20-year olds pretending to be animals. A few hours later, I reversed the process, returned to my office and saw clients. Sometimes I used my office as a rehearsal studio for practice with my scene partner. I can't say my law partners were pleased, but they tolerated it.

Like members of a family, we took responsibility for one another. Although we adopted a results-oriented compensation system based on the dollars we brought to the firm through our initiation of business and the amount we billed and collected for our work, we adjusted the results so that no one faced severe hardship. I was one of the first to benefit from the generosity of my partners: at my first Baker, Weeks board meeting as an outside director, we decided to sell the company, my only client, so that my numbers were very bad that year. I was going to be in financial trouble. My partners bailed me out – this was not a grab-what-you-can world. We had found a different way to run a law firm and over time attracted top graduates from the "best" law schools who were happy to forego the huge salaries and bonuses paid by other prestigious law firms for careers with reasonable compensation and a life outside of work.

Our compensation system gave me the freedom to put my family first. If I did not work as hard or initiate as much business, I took home less money, and within reason that was fine. However, I needed sufficient money to meet the financial obligations of educating Brooke and Blake and helping Rosemary with her career. Since I was not particularly good at marketing myself, there were times when money was much tighter than

I would have wanted. It was not a question of working more because there was no work to be had.

On the non-monetary front, I told my secretary that whenever Brooke or Blake called, she should put the call through to me – no exceptions. No matter if I was in an important meeting with a client, I still wanted the call. It was a two-way street, as evident in the note Brooke wrote to me on my 60th birthday when Bill Clinton was President.

> *When Chelsea Clinton told the school nurse to call her father because her mom was too busy, the world laughed. I knew exactly what she meant.*
> *Can I go to Jocelyn's house? The answer was, call Daddy.*
> *The neighbors are complaining that we're too loud. Call Daddy.*
> *My report card has come, can I open it? Call Daddy.*
> *Yours was the first number I learned after our home,*
> *the place I turned to for advice, permission and conversation.*
> *Other kids' fathers were in meetings. You could always be reached.*
> *For baseball games, trips to Action Park, and the Brearley Christmas assembly, you made the time.*
> *When things got rough in 1983, you took the time to make both children feel wanted. That trip to Nantucket was special.*
> *I remember father-daughter dinners at Lutece and at Odeon, feeling so grown-up.*
> *And how proud I felt when you complimented my car-shopping efforts before you bought my Honda.*
> *When I needed you, you were there. You were my lifeline.*
>
> *Love,*
>
> *Brooke*

Eventually, Brooke and Blake told my secretary not to interrupt me if the matter could wait, but I wanted them to know they were always my first priority.

Despite the uncertainty of my income, for most of my 20 years at Christy & Viener I enjoyed practicing law – and I always muddled through financially. I liked my colleagues, and my clients had interesting issues. I was a creative problem solver. Lawyers in the firm would come to me when they had a problem, whether it was how to get what they wanted in a negotiation, how to keep a deal from cratering, or how to deal with some governmental authority. Clients valued my judgment as much as my legal skills. I got a bit of a reputation negotiating deals where I would get most of what my client wanted and then ask the client whether, given how the other side had acted in the negotiations, my client really wanted to do business with them. The answer was usually no. I saw myself as advancing my clients' long-term interests.

Over time, however, the firm changed. Our happy band of six had grown to 75, and while we had developed an excellent reputation in the legal community, Christy & Viener was no longer the intimate place I had so enjoyed. We had recruited partners who brought business for which we paid them more generously than their old firms. We attracted as associates the best law school graduates who did not want to work the long hours required by the best old-line firms. The culture was changing. Collegiality declined as money-making became the focus. Furthermore, I was also no longer well served by the firm's business model. Compensation was based on hours worked rather than value given, and over time I had become more of an advisor to other lawyers than someone who spent long hours drafting documents. The faster I came up with a helpful solution, the less I was paid.

I became less interested in the firm and in practicing law. I spent some time acting in several Off-Off-Broadway shows and occasionally playing minor roles on daytime soaps. I appeared in some movies produced in New York and in a play in Washington, DC, and became a member of the various unions representing actors. But these distractions were not enough to keep me energized. I tried to add a different dimension to my practice by joining with three former leaders of major enterprises to form a consulting firm specializing in corporate governance - Lear, Yavitz & Associates. But my heart was not in it. It was time to leave the law firm.

I was the first partner to leave Christy & Viener - 20 years to the day after its founding. That says a lot about the culture we had developed. Nonetheless, two years after I left, the firm (no longer controlled by the original six) entered into an ill-fated merger and soon thereafter the C&V lawyers left for other firms. Christy & Viener remains for me the place where I had it all - acceptance and fulfillment at least for the first ten years. I came to understand that the way to achieve my personal goals was by working collaboratively with others and allowing others to attain their own goals - not by being a loner bucking the system as my father believed. I thought I had also learned the importance of shared values, but I needed another lesson to fully incorporate it into my consciousness.

XIV.
Earning a Living

Being 59 and a father with children out of the nest did not relieve me of the need to earn a living. One of the sub-specialties I had developed was representing specialist firms who make the trading markets and execute the transactions on the New York Stock Exchange. My success was such that once when the leaders of two specialist firms decided to merge, each told the other that he had a great lawyer who could do the deal, and it turned out that both were referring to me. I did in fact "do the deal" but only after getting a waiver from both firms and an acknowledgement of exactly what my role would be.

Subsequently, one of my other long-term clients took me to lunch to talk about his move to a new specialist firm. He said that the CEO wanted to take the firm to a higher level but the culture at the firm did not value intelligence. The CEO needed help. I said I would be interested in meeting the CEO, and a dinner was arranged. The CEO and I hit it off, and he had me meet the majority owner who had inherited the firm from his father. That meeting also went well. They asked me to join the firm as Vice Chairman and as a member of the executive committee of the board of directors of the holding company which controlled the specialist firm, a real estate firm, and another securities firm. The executive committee was composed of the two of them and two other managers whom I had met briefly at a lunch.

After a quick negotiation of my compensation, I accepted the offer and joined the firm, Robb, Peck & McCooey. What I learned a few days later was that the two people who hired me had promised the other two on the executive committee that they would not do so – putting me in an untenable position. I had been so keen to leave the law firm that I had not done enough due diligence. I was in the wrong place. All my life I had worked with smart highly educated intelligent people. In this company my education was a strike against me. These were people whose major skills lay in matching buyers and sellers in the frenzy of activity on the stock exchange floor and taking advantage of the moment-to-moment shift in direction of the market. One specialist told me that he saw his career options as working on the floor of the stock exchange or mowing lawns. He was not alone in that attitude. When the firm wanted to raise capital, my education, experience and previous positions had to be scrubbed from the memorandum given to potential investors because it brought into sharp focus the narrow backgrounds of the other senior officers.

Rosemary saw the problem immediately when she met them. We came from different worlds. I wasn't able to bridge the gulf, and they seemed uninterested in trying. The CEO distanced himself from me. I was not welcome. However, I had a contract which paid me nicely if they fired me but not if I resigned. It took two years, but I held on until they fired me. Joining Robb, Peck was a big personal – but not financial – mistake.

In another way the experience was very useful. As Hamlet might have put it, "To err, perchance to learn – ay, there's the gain." I needed to learn to listen, sit back calmly and observe. Anxiety to prove my worth was my undoing. Had I listened, I would never have joined Robb, Peck. But if I had decided to overlook my misgivings, once there I would have handled myself better. Before I joined the firm, I met the principals. I knew our backgrounds were different. Our interests were different. Our values were different. What made me think I could succeed there? Once hired, I did what I thought was right - in terms of instituting practices - without regard to the culture of the firm. Instead of listening and learning how things were done, I imposed my view on company practices. It is unlikely I would have succeeded, but I certainly could have done a better job if I had listened instead of pushing my ideas.

Even though I had been ostracized and fired, I did not feel humiliated as I had at other times when I was rejected. I did not feel bad at all, except that I knew I had not handled myself well. The sizable severance pay I received was certainly a factor, but I think it was more than that. I had come to a place where I knew who I was, and that I was not a bad person. Yes, I needed to become a better listener, but the situation was the problem. I was mature enough to recognize that failure is part of life. I had experienced enough success to give me confidence that I was competent.

Robb, Peck had put some money in my pocket, but not enough to retire. Becoming an active partner in our corporate governance consulting firm Lear, Yavitz was the path of least resistance. It also fit well with the lessons I had learned about the importance of listening. Corporate governance consulting – working with boards of directors – is all about listening, drawing directors out so that their issues can be openly addressed. Part of the job of listening is letting the directors know they have been heard – and understood. Only when they know they are understood are they ready to listen.

My colleagues asked me to be the managing partner of the consulting firm – not an honor unless you think being responsible for finding clients without a monetary incentive is an honor. They were happy to do the consulting – the fun part – but none of them wanted to do the marketing. I understood.

After two years of modest results, I resigned and joined another consulting firm specializing in organizational change which wanted to build its corporate governance consulting practice. The firm had an interesting culture. They wanted their professionals to understand all aspects of their business. Consequently, my first year at the firm was spent primarily as a student, learning about the various aspects of organizational change. Unfortunately at the end of that year – a bad year for their consulting business – they dismissed almost everybody who had just completed the training.

Given my background, no one thought they would let me go. But they didn't know what I knew. I wasn't good for the CEO's ego. He had taken me with him to show me how to properly interview a director. Unfortunately, the director he chose was Nick Nicholas a longtime good friend of mine. When Nick greeted us, almost before the CEO could get a word out, Nick told the CEO how lucky he was to have me on board. My position was further compromised by the fact that I was quoted in newspapers more often than the CEO. That was only natural since I had been in the corporate governance field much longer than he had, but I know it rankled him. In any event, I was laid off with the others. I didn't feel bad about it – it just wasn't my scene.

Even at this late age, 65, I was not mature enough to keep

a low profile. I was still intent on establishing my own identity and credentials. For over 30 years I had been my own boss. Like my father I was too independent for corporate life. The irony was that my father saw success as achieving a high position in a large corporate organization – but he had raised me to be skeptical of authority and my own approach to dealing with an unfriendly world made me unfit for such a life. I wasn't an organization man, I had to work for myself.

Lear, Yavitz was no more, so for lack of another ready option, I started Masters Governance Consulting. At about that time, my friend Carolyn Brancato who had promoted my corporate governance credentials at The Conference Board invited me to her wedding in Maryland. On the way, I stopped off at a gas station to get directions and met another wedding guest who was lost, Alan Rudnick who, it turned out, was also doing corporate governance consulting. We were seated next to each other at the wedding and became friendly. A month or so later, Alan was chairing a program for The Conference Board's Directors Institute, and I turned up (having been invited by Carolyn) to be one of the opening speakers.

My talk apparently impressed one of the participants who asked if I might be interested in doing some consulting work for Avon. I also learned that Alan was being considered. Here, Alan's and my version of events conflict. Alan says he called me. I say I called him. We agree, however, that the substance of the call was that Avon offered enough work for both of us and we agreed to work together. We did and have ever since, but it was three years of working together through our separate entities before we formed one company, Masters-Rudnick & Associates, our flagship, where we have worked seamlessly for the last ten years – a true partnership. I could not have asked for a more compatible business partner.

Helping boards to be more effective is a business I really enjoy and which utilizes my skills and experience. I get to work with bright people who make their own decisions on issues they personally care about – no bureaucracy and no receivables problem. Because professional satisfaction has always been my quest, when something did not work out, I went on to the next thing. Resilience and perseverance had become second nature to me – a consequence of needing to succeed when the odds were against me as a child. My father can take some credit for that with his demands that I excel in circumstances made more difficult by the family secret.

XV.
Matters of Substance

When my mother was 100 years old, I wrote her the following note which I had framed as an early Mothers' Day present in 2007.

Remembrances for my Mother who always did her very best

I remember when I was sick, you cared for me and brought me comics.

I remember how you always showed up at school in your Nurse's Aide uniform, and I was so proud of you.

I remember how you would come to my soccer games, and the endless series of school plays which you sat through.

I remember the times you took me to Hamburger Heaven and Chock Full O' Nuts and my favorite, Schrafft's, after school.

I remember shopping with you until you were sure that I had the very best fitting blue blazers and grey slacks at the lowest available prices.

I remember going to the movies with you on Thursday nights and your making candy.

I remember your concern for my physical health – a concern that continues today.

I remember how you helped me get ads for my high school yearbook.

I remember how you reached out to welcome Rosemary into the family.

I remember how you helped her in matters of dress and appearance and gave her the confidence to feel at home in the sophisticated New York world.

I remember how you arranged for our honeymoon trip to Bermuda.

I remember your sending us to London with instructions – and money - for a Savile Row tailor to make me two double-breasted pinstriped suits, making sure my legal career would begin on a well-dressed note.

I remember many other good things as well, but most of all, I remember how you cared.

Love,

Jon

We were in her den. She was very pleased and read it over and over, gushing about what a good mother she had been. The phone rang. It was Kim, and I turned away to answer it. We talked for a few minutes but when I turned to hand her the phone, my mother had had a stroke. That note was the last thing she ever read.

It had been a long time since I had done something that pleased her. We had a difficult relationship – I wanted more than she could give. She wanted more than I could give. Her parenting focused on surface characteristics like how I looked or what clothes I wore. If I brought up an intellectual or cultural issue, she changed the subject. She liked to describe in great detail the "swell" parties she attended, what everyone wore, what was served for dinner, and who she sat next to. When I asked what that person did or said, she claimed not to remember.

She had always talked about how much she liked the 1920's – elegant parties, beautiful clothes, fun dances. In an effort to engage her, in my junior year at Princeton I wrote a paper comparing Fitzgerald, Dos Passos, and Hemingway and their works describing the Twenties which I thought would interest her. She refused even to read it. She said she wouldn't understand it and would not even try. My feelings were hurt, but I realized that because of her poor education, she was painfully insecure and terrified of looking stupid.

We did fun things together when I was a little boy, but I wanted – needed – a deeper emotional connection. I wanted a mother I could talk to, who would understand, advise, and commiserate. Harriet, the nanny I loved, was gone. Neglected emotionally as a child, my mother could not relate to my needs and was incapable of responding to my feelings. Like all children, I wanted to know about my mother's past - her experiences growing up, what her parents were like, what prompted my parents to get married seven days after they met - and I hoped she would share the memories of her life as an older, wiser woman. She wouldn't, or more likely couldn't. When I asked her about the ordinary issues of the day, she never expressed any opinions of her own. She simply repeated what she heard some friend say, and if I suggested an alternative opinion, she cut off the discussion with "Well, that's the way it is." I knew she lacked an intellectual background and did not want to look stupid, but no matter how hard I tried to understand, I took her evasiveness as rejection and withdrew from her emotionally– not physically, I continued to see her. The lack of substantive discussions or conversations affected my own intellectual development: I was not challenged to – and for many years did not - think in depth about anything.

As my mother grew older, she held me at arm's length – which I decided was her way of maintaining her independence. She had a life of her own. She was a regular theatregoer and was always accompanying "friends" whom she refused to name. And as in my childhood, she never talked to me about the plays she had seen.

I wish I could say that my grateful Mothers' Day remembrance was a successful peace offering and that all ended well between us, but it didn't. My mother had told me that she wanted to die in her apartment, but when she had the stroke, I called 911 for an ambulance. When the Emergency Medical Team arrived, she stretched both arms out at her sides in an attempt to prevent them from taking her through the doorways to Lenox Hill Hospital. I was not going to let her die in the hospital, but I could not deny her the chance of recovery. After a few days in the hospital it became clear that my mother would not recover, and I brought her home where she had round-the-clock care. She died in her sleep seven weeks later. I visited her every day, but she refused to recognize my presence and turned her head away. She did not want to see me. That was hard. I am not sure what my mother wanted from me – perhaps she expected her children to heal her own childhood wounds, and she was angry we didn't. Whatever it was, what I could give was not enough. I still regret that I was not mature enough to accept my mother for who she was. That pogrom in Russia had devastated her family and deprived her of the love and attention she should have had. She had done her best, but I had wanted so much more.

If she had failed me emotionally, she had unwittingly secured my financial security and my brother's as well by persuading my father to buy the apartment I grew up in. The initial offering price in 1940 was $12,000 which my father thought was outrageous, but by the time, six months later, my mother convinced him to buy, he had to pay $18,000. I knew the apartment would be the major asset in my mother's estate, and I had been thinking about the best way to realize enough money on it for my brother and me to have comfortable retirements. My mother had told me that whatever I did, I should not sell the apartment to the first bidder. Typically, she adopted a point of view with no regard for the context. In fact, the context dictated otherwise. I would have to take a different approach.

A year or two before my mother died – she was in good health at the time – I happened to sit opposite her upstairs neighbor at a black tie dinner. After dinner he took me aside and made a proposal. He would like to buy the apartment from my mother at the appraised price and let her live there free for the rest of her life. I told him that would not make sense because of the large capital gains taxes she would have to pay on the sale and second because the balance would be taxed again in her estate. However, I took note of his desire for the apartment.

I realized that my mother's apartment would be worth more to him than a similar stand-alone apartment. He and his wife were determined to enlarge their apartment and buying my mother's apartment was the only way they could do it. I had learned from Roger Fisher, cemented by own experience negotiating transactions, that successful negotiators focus on understanding the perspective of the person with whom they are negotiating. In this case, the cost of the apartment was an issue only in so far as the potential buyer would not want to feel ripped off. Given that I wanted an extremely high price – one that I had learned was not inappropriate for such an in-house purchase – I needed to create a situation where buying the apartment at my price was his choice, not something I had forced him to do. In that way I thought I could complete the deal on terms satisfactory to both of us

Here's what I did. When my mother died, I called the potential buyer, her upstairs neighbor. His office said he was on a flight to London and I replied that he would want to know that I was going to put my mother's apartment on the market. Within a few hours he called me from Heathrow airport. I told him that I would be willing to sell the apartment for what I considered a good price. He pointed out it was higher than the general market price for that type of apartment. "I would be happy to negotiate," I said, "but then I would also make the apartment available to other possible buyers, including the downstairs neighbor." It was his choice. Did he want to pay my price, or negotiate and risk losing the apartment to someone else who bid higher? I gave him a deadline and a short while later, he called to say he would take the apartment at my price. We had an oral handshake, and that was that. It took a month or so before we had anything in writing, but neither of us had any question that it was a done deal.

A few months after the closing, the buyer and his wife – thoughtfully anticipating our interest - asked Rosemary and me to see how they had redone the apartment, and whenever I see the buyer, he is very friendly. Mission accomplished – both parties satisfied. That felt good.

XVI.
Winning the Lottery

The lottery of life depends on so much we cannot control – genetics, environment, happenstance and luck. We were lucky. Blake told me, "Dad, you won the lottery and you don't know it." He was wrong – I knew before he said it. When he was 13, he told me "You did a terrible thing. You made us internalize your values." What more can a father want. I'm sure my father wanted it, and maybe he would be pleased with the way I turned out. But we conducted ourselves so differently that I doubt he would have recognized that we had similar goals. We both wanted a close-knit nuclear family, rewarding careers for our children and ourselves, and acceptance from people we liked and admired. His approach was to try to enforce his will on his children, mine was to encourage and support them to be their own persons. Moreover, given the widespread anti-Semitism at the time, he did not trust the system to treat him fairly. His dictate –"Never stand on line"– may have made sense for him but not for me who had grown up among upper class Christians at a time when anti-Semitism was waning.

For Rosemary and me, internalizing our personal values meant being good and loving people, prizing family, working hard and persevering to achieve your goals. We cherish other values as well like making the world – or that part we can influence – a better place, but in my hierarchy the personal ones have priority.

Our standards were high. Life – with two parents who graduated from Harvard Law School and had problems of their own – was not easy for Brooke and Blake. They knew we loved them, but as Blake said, "We know you would love us if we got Ds, but it is just assumed we will get As." That pressure sometimes made them very hard on themselves and led to other difficulties. Paradoxically, I did not make things easier by constantly praising them – a knee jerk reaction to the fact that my father had never praised me. Rosemary cautioned me that my praise was adding to the pressure, but I was deaf to her advice. Blake tells me that as a high school student he engaged in some risky behavior which he assures me "I am too young to know about."

Yet Blake was right. They had internalized Rosemary's and my values – choosing loving and supporting partners, supporting and encouraging their children, and succeeding in challenging careers. Moreover, they even gave us some credit. These are notes I received.

On my 70th birthday, Brooke wrote

Things My Father Taught Me

To aim high and try my best
To watch for windows in the wine and drink great bottles on great occasions
That Berkshire mud beats Hampton beach, hands down
To love the theatre and sing the show tunes – loudly
To take on any challenge

That math is fun for everyone – girls included
To greet each day as an opportunity and not dwell on yester-
day's troubles
To value family with all of its complications, craziness and love
That the most important part of parenting is being there to listen

Brooke Masters,
June 2007

Blake on giving me a framed collage of pictures celebrating the first season of his television series *Brotherhood* and my appearance on the series as the Governor of Rhode Island:

For: The Governor,

A memento of your first (and hopefully not last) term of office.
It makes me happy that I could share my success with you,
for without your love + support, none of it would've been
possible.

Love,

Blake

My highest priority has been being a good father, and nothing has brought me more satisfaction. Their chosen partners, John and Missy, have further enriched my life and brought me great joy. As John might say in a Minnesota compliment, "A father and a father-in-law could do worse."

But there would have been no winning of the lottery without Rosemary. She has been my spur and support, my partner in giving our children the love and care they deserve, my best friend and lover, and my example in making the world a better place. Yet, our marriage has not always been easy. There was my early inability to have any kind of intellectual discussion without turning it into combat and all the other consequences of maintaining the family secret. Rosemary, too, struggled with issues that went back to her childhood. Both of us were and are determined and forceful in presenting our views. Disagreements were expected and conflict was inevitable. Rosemary once went off on her own to Jackson Hole to sort things out for what was supposed to be three weeks. I took each of the children on a trip – Brooke to the beaches of Nantucket, Blake to the mountains of Colorado. Rosemary came home early, and together we worked to resolve our issues.

Through it all though there was no question that we shared the same basic values. I had never accepted my parents' belief that life was about appearance and self-satisfaction. Because I didn't have to fight as hard as they did to get what I wanted, I could afford to "stand on line." I knew my turn would come. I wanted to be seen as an individual and not as a member of a group – *i.e.*, a Jew - and I viewed others the same way – on their individual merits. My teachers at St. Bernard's and Exeter helped shape my values with their emphasis on ethics and social responsibility. Rosemary and I loved each other and were determined to make our marriage work. We kiss a lot. Affection is important even when – *especially* when – you disagree. We have been married for more than 52 years, and as we have matured, we have truly become best friends and lovers.

I have framed in my office the notes we exchanged on our 60th birthdays.

To Jon on His 60th Birthday

I remember the day we met. We were first year students at Harvard Law School. You sat behind me in property class. When you asked me what I was doing for Thanksgiving, I thought, "What a nice smile and what an elegant tweed sport jacket." You still have that warm smile and you still have that same elegance. You may even have the same tweed jacket!

I remember the day of my first moot court competition. I was scared to death because I had to make a legal argument before what seemed a terrifyingly smart third year student. You gave me a yellow rose and told me not to worry. You've given me yellow roses ever since to cheer me on whenever I had a big professional challenge before me. You were a feminist before anyone we knew even mentioned that word. You always helped me believe in myself and you encouraged me to use my mind and talents in the world as your equal – even if you still don't know where I keep the windex.

I remember the nights when Brooke and Blake had the croup. We took turns sitting with them for hours in the bathroom with the shower steaming. I sang songs; you told them stories about Tug Boat Annie. You were always my partner. We shared not just the joys but the worries and responsibilities. One reason my life could be as full as it has been is that both children could turn to you for comfort and advice when I couldn't be there.

I remember the day that Gilbert, our Yorkshire terrier, got lost. You searched up and down the highway for hours and knocked on dozens of doors until you found him. You refused to give up. That search was so like you – stubbornly loyal, determined to protect those you love no matter what.

I remember six golden Fall days in Rome when we were so very young and just out of law school. We explored the Forum, drank frascatti wine and delighted in the beauty of the world and each other. Despite some stormy interludes, our life together has been like those matchless days – full of sensual pleasure, exciting adventures and good company. We have been and still are in the very truest sense of the words, both friends and lovers.

All my love,

Rosemary

For My Love on Her 60ᵗʰ Birthday

When you turned around between Contracts and Property wide-eyed and in need of a good haircut, I was immediately attracted, but I had no idea what I was getting into - or how lucky I was. Underneath that look of innocence was a woman of depth with a piercing intellect, a fierce determination and an extraordinary capacity for loving and caring. Our lives have since been bound together by the joys we have shared, the disappointments we have survived, the battles we have fought, the love we have made, and the children we have nurtured. I would have it no other way. I love you. Happy birthday.

Jon

Our family in the Berkshires, c. 1983

XVII.
Sharing My Life Lessons

Looking back, I realize that my greatest source of joy has been helping others succeed –as a parent, a counsellor, or a mentor. Being a good father has brought the greatest reward. Our children are caring and accomplished adults with whom we have a loving relationship. In my various careers – in government, politics, urban renewal, law, the securities industry, and corporate governance – I was an advisor, often the principal advisor, to the person in charge – and always gave what I thought was my best advice without regard to whether my advisee wanted to hear it. My acting had taught me how to connect with people and win their trust: be in the moment, listen, get out of my head, react with my whole body – basics for any actor.

Acting was an integral part of my life: my passion, and part of the assignment from my parents – play a part – preserve the secret, and they, perhaps unwittingly, encouraged me to find the tools to succeed at that task. By regularly taking me to Broadway shows, which I loved, and reacting uncritically when I announced as a six year old that I wanted to be an actor, they made acting safe for me – a haven where they would not interfere. I was allowed to enter into another world – no appearances to keep up – just be – no pressure. I made new friends – people I would not normally meet in my social or business circles – in the rehearsal process; although when the show closed or the scene class was over, we usually went our separate ways. While I was rejected far more often than I was selected for a part in my 40s and 50s, I didn't feel the system was stacked against me as I did in other parts of my life – that's what auditions are for. I would try again – my perseverance was ingrained. When it came to acting, I was in charge of my life.

Acting spurred my curiosity – it was imaginative play. I could be anybody I wanted to be. I could give in to my emotions – and I did. I remember playing Brutus in *Julius Caesar* and feeling like a "big man" because it was the largest part and the action of the play depended on my decisions. As Tony Lumpkin in *She Stoops to Conquer*, I unleashed my wild teenager self when I stole my mother's jewels and slid across the stage knocking down the scenery. If I messed up, the worst consequence would a bad review. One of my proudest moments on the stage was when I was playing the Vice President's national security advisor in a play based on the advisor's testimony before a Senate subcommittee, and one member of the audience who had actually questioned the advisor came up to me after the performance with the compliment that my hand gestures were just like the advisor's. Whether they were or not, I have no idea, but I had researched the character as I often did and even talked to his previous employer. Perhaps I had learned enough to mirror the character that he could imagine that I made similar hand gestures.

Acting was much more than training and performing though

I love that too: just this last January I went to Shakespeare boot camp – a training intensive for professional actors at Shakespeare & Company in Lenox, Massachusetts, 14 hours a day, 6 days a week, for 4 weeks – so exhausting and exhilarating that I lost 14 pounds, but also affirming of my ability and my decision not be an actor as a career – no way to have a stable marriage or raise a family. Acting had different purposes at different times: as a schoolboy, I could be a star and forget that I was two years younger than my classmates. I also hoped that acting would give me an emotional connection with my mother who came to my plays, but she was unable to talk about the play or my performance. As a young adult, I learned how to present myself as a confident, articulate companion and colleague. As a lawyer, I honed my ability to persuade, and when I was tiring of law practice, I tried to reenergize by spending Thursday afternoons in grueling acting classes with a lot of enthusiastic kids and beginning to audition again.

Working with colleagues who were emotionally open and exploring the characters I played taught me a lot about people. With its emphasis on how we present ourselves and how we relate to one another, some exposure to acting is probably a worthwhile pursuit for everyone. It's said that those who choose an acting career do so only because it is the only thing they wanted. That wasn't my feeling, but a passion for acting greatly enriched my life. If – when – you find a passion, don't dismiss it – tread gently. It could be your key to fulfillment.

People often ask me to mentor them. At one point, my mentees ranged from successful business women and men to young entrepreneurs to college students – ranging in age from 18 to 52. It was my version of Exeter's *non sibi*. They enriched my world, and I expanded theirs. Many of the students came from

Eastern Europe with their careers planned in advance. Before I got them to expand their horizons, they were intent on taking only courses and internships directly related to those careers. I was able to show them how limiting that approach to life could be and how much my career has been the product of happenstance. As the range of their experiences increased, they found themselves with more opportunities than they ever imagined. Some changed careers, others found new interests.

Many of my mentees, particularly the college students, were also moving to a world foreign to their parents, an experience not so different from my own, though mine had not been handicapped by poverty. My life had been far easier, but just as different from my grandparents' lives as those of most of my students were from their parents' lives. Helping my mentees adjust to their new surroundings and maintain their family connections was a learning experience for me as well as them.

Frankly, I find my greatest rewards in mentoring extremely bright and talented individuals who might well succeed without my help. I am sure I make their paths a bit smoother, but I often wonder if I should be focusing more on those who are less gifted. However, because I am more successful in working with bright people, I decided some time ago that my mentoring would have more impact if I helped change the lives of leaders, who could then pass their knowledge on to the less able or fortunate. Is this decision self-serving? Perhaps, but I'm doing what I do best.

I have recently been given the opportunity to mentor some high potential LaGuardia Community College students who come from difficult and deprived circumstances. In trying to help them realize their goals, I plan to share with them these lessons from my life:

Take charge of your life – don't let others define you. You're en-titled. Don't live someone else's dream. My father took charge of his life, and from my point of view, the results were, in some ways, less successful for him than they were for me. But even as he provided me with creature comforts, financial security and even challenges, he also stunted my intellectual and emotional growth. Fathers owe their children love and care, but they are not entitled to take charge of their lives and he wasn't entitled to take charge of mine.

Set priorities – know where you are going. Decide what matters to you and go after it. Don't be afraid to make choices, you are young you can change them. I did – even after 30 years when I revealed the secret, chose fatherhood over career, gave up imagined possibilities of success and power for a loving family life. These were not easy decisions, but they were the right ones for me. It is true that from time to time I think about the fact that I have not sought public renown, but given what that would have involved, I doubt I would have been successful. I have some regrets, but the path I chose has brought me great joy.

Don't put blinders on. The world will change. You'll change. Adapt. Don't be like my father who saw life though a narrow small town lens, didn't recognize that he could succeed as a Jew, and later missed the fact that the world had changed and was becoming less ant-Semitic. He was blind to the possibility that abandoning the secret might allow him to have a more ful-filling life.

Allow for happenstance. The unexpected will happen: my de-sire to play catch on a fall evening led to a NROTC scholarship; my knowledge of Faulkner led to politico-military policy as-signments in the Pentagon; my going to a football game led to Harvard law School and Rosemary; and on and on. You may get lucky. Take advantage of it. I certainly did.

Aim high and do your best. Doing your best means working hard. "99 is not 100," my father taught me. It is not just a matter of one point. It is a matter of determination - your commitment to succeed. But working hard is not enough if you don't work intelligently – it's not the hours spent, it's the results.

Be willing to take risks. Allow yourself to be different – to follow your vision. But don't lose touch with reality. We all have different levels of risk tolerance. Learn yours.

Develop all your senses. Be curious intellectually – my early failing – but make sure you are in touch with your emotions. My emotional sensibilities and warmth have been the linchpins of my marriage. My experiences as an actor have not only taught me to deal with rejection, they have helped me understand emotions – mine and that of others. Take part in art and participate in cultural activities – these can also foster happiness and creativity.

Learn to listen. If you're talking you're not learning. Hear what others have to say. You don't have all the answers. There's an added reward: listening helps to disarm your adversary in a negotiation.

Be open with your loved ones. Secrets are toxic and destroy your vitally important emotional connections.

Get others to help you. Develop networks. Find mentors. Much as they may want to be, many parents are not good or sufficient mentors, unfamiliar with the environment in which their children are trying to thrive. I lucked in to my mentors; you may have to search for them. But don't be afraid to ask someone to mentor you; they'll be flattered even if they decide not to take you on.

Maintain relationships – don't burn bridges. I didn't do very well on this score – to my everlasting regret. Recognize that you and your parents are living in very different worlds: they may often be confused by yours, and you may be irritated by theirs. Neither world has all the answers, and you should be ready to take what is important from both and remain part of the family.

Learn from your mistakes – but don't let them demoralize you. Don't just write off mistakes; focus on them; think about what could have been done differently; and remember it for the next time. My father was terrified and angry when I made mistakes. The lesson I had to unlearn was "mistakes mean you're stupid and unlovable; mistakes are unforgivable." Hopefully I am learning how wrong that is.

Help others. Share what you've learned with others. Do what was done for you. That is the way we build a better society. But don't think of it as a sacrifice, because it is truly more rewarding to give than to receive – I can bear witness.

Persevere. You are not going to succeed all the time. I have been fired twice. Once because I made a really stupid decision; the other time because I was a bad fit for the job and should never have taken it in the first place. What's so bad about rejection? As an actor, you get used to it and in the end it improves your work. The key is to get up and try again and again – and again. As Winston Churchill said, "When you are going through hell, keep going." No one is going to hand you happiness or success. Real success comes from perseverance.

Chronology

June 20, 1937 – I am born.

September, 1942 - June, 1950 – St. Bernard's School

December 9, 1947 – My father's mother, Rose Moskowitz dies.

Spring, 1948   We leave the family.

September, 1950 - June, 1954 – Exeter

September, 1954 - June, 1958 – Princeton

June, 1958 - December, 1959 – USS Northampton (CLC-1)

January, 1960 - June 1961 – Op61 (CNO's Politico-Military Policy staff)

June, 1961 - August, 1961 – Sea level canal study with Gardner Ackley for Army UnderSecretary

September, 1961 - June, 1964 – Harvard Law School

June 16, 1962 – Married Rosemary Cox

June, 1962 - September, 1962 – Policy Planning staff of Assistant Secretary of Defense/ISA

December, 1962 - June, 1964 – Research Assistant to Roger Fisher

June, 1964 - November, 1964 – Pres. Johnson's Political Research staff

November, 1964 - December, 1964 – European trip to remember

January, 1965 - June, 1968 – Shearman & Sterling

July 28, 1967 – Brooke is born

June, 1968 - June, 1969 – Bedford-Stuyvesant Corporation

June, 1969 - November, 1969 – Shearman & Sterling

November, 1969 - June, 1976 – Baker, Weeks & Co., Inc.

November 11, 1970 – Blake is born

July, 1976 - June, 1996 – Christy & Viener

Summer, 1979 – We rejoin the family.

July, 1996 - August, 1998 – Robb, Peck & McCooey

September, 1998 - June, 2001 – Lear, Yavitz & Associates

June, 2001 - June, 2002 – Mercer Delta

June, 2002 - September, 2005 – Masters Governance Consulting

October, 2005 - Present – Masters-Rudnick & Associates

Afterword

By

Dr. Kim J. Masters

I was honored when my brother asked me to write an after-word to this compelling memoir. I am proud to acknowledge the great contribution that Jon has made to my life, my personal development, and the welfare of my family. I regret that I did not always take advantage of opportunities for us to work or be together.

As you read the memoir, you will recognize Jon's strength of character and commitment to help others, especially his family. I believe his difficulties with Mother and Dad were not of his own making, but an outgrowth of the personal decisions that limited our parents' friendships and promoted fiat in place of discussion. They also failed to appreciate Jon's innate intelligence. He was intellectually sharper than anyone else in the family.

I experienced Mother and Dad as Scylla and Charybdis, the mythic guardians of a dangerous strait viewed by the Greeks as twin evils, their volume amplified in unnecessary and destructive arguments with Jon. Throughout my childhood and early adulthood, I believed that peace was best achieved by keeping quiet and hoping for the best. Jon correctly realized that confronting their edicts was a more useful way of dealing with them. Of course, he knew about the family's Jewish history and I was not told about it until I was 30 years old. As long as Jon was there to object to my parents' controlling behavior, I felt less need to confront them. Nevertheless, the results of this need to control, born apparently from their fear of being exposed as Jews, was evident in almost everything they did. I think it played a role in their decision to switch me from St. Bernard's, where I was happy, to Buckley, where I had to repeat the fourth grade – although their stated reason was that St. Bernard's was not demanding enough of me because I was Jon's brother and he had excelled there. I also think that the odd ways they tried to control my behavior, and their refusal to discuss political or cultural events, played a role in my interest about the Holocaust as I was growing up. From what Jon has told me the "secret" was hatched when I was a year old and lasted more than a quarter century. However, as any family therapist will tell you, those unaware of their family history, often sense it unconsciously and act it out. This was succinctly stated by the philosopher George Santayana in a famous quotation which I saw on a sign hanging at the exit to Dachau in 1967: "Those who cannot remember the past [or do not know it] are condemned to repeat it." (<u>Reason and Common Sense</u>, volume 1, p. 284, 1905.) The addiction recovery mantra: "You are as sick as your secrets," similarly addresses the toxicity of secrets. In my case, parental secrecy and lack of any kind of meaningful conversation about current events created such a consuming interest in the extermination of the Jews that in my early twenties I sought to meet the only surviving member of Hitler's entourage.

Another difficulty was that I was given a girl's name. I later wondered if this gender confusion was connected to my interest in listening to conversations. Actually my birth name was James Kim, but I think my mother, who tried to make reality conform to her wishes, changed it to Kim James. (Perhaps she wanted a girl?) I was told I was named after Rudyard Kipling's hero Kim, a boy, a vagrant and a spy in the heyday of the Raj. I doubt Mother read the book. She told me I was born after she saw pictures of the devastation of Hiroshima. These disparate and disconnected pieces of information suggested that I had disappointed her by being born a boy, and that my birth was somehow connected to a terrible disaster. In retrospect these revelations reflected two different family story lines. In addition to its female connections the name Kim seemed at the time more appropriate for a child than a man, making it easier for my mother to delay my maturity by dressing me in shorts when all my classmates were wearing long pants, and also by postponing my shaving by taking me to a wax salon to remove that early sign of puberty - a moustache. Whatever the case, the bombing of Hiroshima came to metaphorically symbolize my parents abrupt rejection of all their Jewish friends and family (except for Uncle Walter) and the loss of communication with their past.

Hiroshima had another terrifying meaning for me: somehow I connected it with a throat infection that almost killed me when I was five years old. This illness occurred almost simultaneously with the death of my close friend who accidentally shot himself with his grandfather's gun. My mother's insistence that the doctor come to our house at midnight and take me to the hospital undoubtedly saved my life. Whatever her flaws, she saw me through a terrifying tracheotomy and stayed with me at the hospital for a week, and I would never forget it This near-death experience had a lot to do with my choosing a career in medicine. It also left me with a persistent fear about having just barely survived, and I became more anxious than other boys. The anxiety revealed itself in nervous questioning in classes and assemblies that annoyed both teachers and my peers.

I never saw my maternal grandfather, although he lived until I was 10 years old. I believe I was taken to see my maternal grandmother once but remember only that someone gave me a brown and yellow toy bus to play with. Years later when I asked mother whom we had visited, she told me, "A friend who had moved to California."

A few years later, I opened up Uncle Walter's war-time suitcase, stored in the basement, found a Nazi flag and put it up on my wall. Mother tore it down without explanation. I thought I had done something wrong, but no explanation was forth coming.

In high school I ran a film festival, and the one film that fascinated me was Alain Resnais's *Nuit et Brouillard* : "Night and Fog" (1955) about Nazi concentration camps which asks the question " Who is responsible?," The answer from everyone was " Not me, I was following orders." I thought it would be simple to identify the monster who exterminated six million Jews, but everyone seemed to have had an excuse. According to Hanna Arendt's report of his 1960 trial for crimes against humanity in Jerusalem in 1960, Eichmann, the enforcer of the Final Solution said, "He had no dislike for Jews; he was carrying out a plan given to him by his superiors; he had no regrets, because he executed it efficiently despite many logistical disruptions." I believe that *Nuit et Brouillard* ends with "We are all responsible." It must be true because we still have genocide repeating itself: Kosovo, Rwanda, South Sudan, Syria.

Then there was the Hunters Point incident. Mother, Dad and I had gotten off the Southampton to New York train one Sunday evening. In those days, the train stopped at Hunters Point Avenue, requiring a transfer to a private car or cab. We were travelling with a well-heeled but inebriated Social Register friend. He spied a limousine with an elegantly dressed, elderly passenger. When the driver said that he could not take 5 passengers, this presumed pillar of society dragged the man from the car, called him a "Dirty Jew," and left him standing on the sidewalk. Following his command to get in the car and without discussion then or later, we drove off. I was frightened by this experience at the time, but was not accustomed to confront adults and was afraid that if I did say something, my father would have reacted with rage, or at the very least, given me a dirty look. Was he upset about this man's behavior but afraid to object because he was afraid any reaction might reveal him as a Jew? I will never know, but I never forgot my own discomfort and bewilderment at the time.

Whenever I asked about the family, Dad would say they were Lutherans. After our Episcopalian minister, Rev. Kinsolving, encouraged me to think about the ministry as a career, Dad told me that he had thought about becoming an Episcopal minister himself. I thought this was wonderful, and it afforded me a singular opportunity to ask about his religious feelings and beliefs, but the occasion passed. Maybe he wanted to let me know he liked Rev. Kinsolving? My father never showed any interest in in Anglican theology or the mystical elements in the religion. More likely he thought the label "Episcopalian" served his personal goals better than "Jewish"?

In medical school, I did something which today strikes me

as naïve, and extraordinarily brash. I asked in a letter to inter-view Albert Speer, Hitler's munitions' minister, in his house in Heidelberg. For reasons I don't fully understand even today, he agreed. I had read his book on Hitler and thought that I could get a firsthand answer to the question "Why didn't someone stop the Holocaust?" It seemed to me that his book provided important insights into the failings of the Third Reich, and that he came across as a "truthful, nice sort of person."

Thus after graduation in 1972, I visited Herr Speer at his home in the hills above Heidelberg. He and his wife were very gracious to me, and welcomed me with cake and coffee. I asked Speer about his book on Hitler. He told me, quite specifically, that if during the Holocaust, I had asked him to stop the exter-minations in the camps, he would have told me it was not his job. He claimed to have cared about the suffering of the prison-ers and showed me photos of the prisoners who worked in his factories pointing out how well fed they were. He also claimed he hadn't known about the exterminations. Twenty-five years later I learned from Gita Sereny's book, <u>Albert Speer: His Battle with Truth,</u> he was at a meeting where Himmler discussed the "Final Solution". When asked why killing women and children was necessary, Himmler reportedly replied, "So they do not come back and get revenge".

I still have notes from my interview with Albert Speer and the friendly self-serving letters he wrote to me. He was charm-ing and at the time I took him at his word. Today I know such skills are the staples of con men, psychopaths and narcissists. I don't know if Albert Speer was any of these, or just someone try-ing to cover up his crimes. Dad was curious about my visit with Speer – not the details of our meeting – just that I had met with him. He even mentioned my interview to John Toland, author of a well-known biography of Hitler, whom he had met at a lecture. However, neither he nor mother ever discussed their feelings about the Nazis or the Holocaust. It would have been an interesting conversation, they would have had to acknowledge the history of persecution, the role of fear as the basis of their conversion. On the other hand, their desire for success, money and acceptance in Park Avenue Society seemed the stronger motive. The only time I ever heard my parents mention Jews was when my father felt cheated by a store owner and muttered that the owner was a "Dirty Jew."

When Geraldine and I started dating, she and I discussed what the family might be hiding. She remembers my thinking we had a serial killer on our family tree.

One of the most confusing aspects of my upbringing was my parents' concern about my posture and whether my pants pockets were free of keys. They also objected to my wearing glasses which I really needed. Mother was preoccupied with my glasses; Dad with my pockets. Geraldine stopped the latter, when she suggested that bulky pants pockets signaled great fertility.

Interpreting these obsessions years later after I had learned the secret meant understanding that glasses and baggy pants and posture were not part of the WASP image. Intelligence did not count for much, so I guess my parents preferred a well-dressed nearsighted Christian to an intellectual Jew.

Another later and equally confusing element of the secret was Dad's fierce anger following its revelation. I remember a family lunch at Tavern on the Green, with Jon and Rosemary, Geraldine, Brooke and Blake, Mother and Dad which was disrupted by Dad's uncontrolled rage. He addressed Jon and Rosemary with remarks like, "I don't hate you, I just don't like you," while telling me, "I'm sorry that you have to see all this." Brooke and Blake, age 9 and 6, as I remember, managed to flee the table for the bathroom, and Mother in a futile attempt at distraction offered, "There is interesting painting on the cornices of the ceiling." I only said, "That's fine with me," when I should have confronted him with my real feelings: "I wish you would stop being angry so we can have a pleasant meal." The revelation of the secret undermined Dad's sense of control as Jon has written.

Meals seemed to offer Dad the best opportunity for being unpleasant or just nasty. Maybe paying for meals provided financial justification for anger at unappreciative sons - like his distorted version of the Golden Rule, "He who has the gold, makes the rules." He also refused to let either Jon or me take him to dinner, saying, "If you pay for a meal with me that will be the last meal we have together." There is obviously a great deal of family history behind Dad's need to control and verbal outburst at meals. We can only guess what dinner at our grandparents' home had been like. We will never know.

In retrospect, however dysfunctional our family appears, I had enjoyed many financial and social benefits. I have no idea what would have happened, if there had never been a secret. Would I would have grown up without a career in medicine which is what I cherish most, or without the social awkwardness that often left me hurt and bewildered as a child? Would I have chosen to become a child psychiatrist or gone on to a career in physical medicine? I still harbor guilt for my silence when I witnessed cruelty committed for three seats in a limousine. I also would have been better served if I had tried to discuss our parents' outrageous behavior with Jon. He was so much older than I was, and away in the Navy or at school when I was a teenager that such opportunities were limited. With no idea that there was a "secret" I was left to puzzle over the outbursts, to wonder why my father behaved as he did. I once asked Uncle Walter about our family background, but he simply put me off and told me to ask our parents.

I don't remember any time when everyone in the family was happy at the same time. Someone was always wrong or inadequate, usually Jon or me. This attitude may have helped me in evaluating illness, but it is hardly ideal for collaboration or the "warm fuzzies" families enjoy.

I always appreciated Rosemary's support when I was teenager, and later her interest in sharing her extensive knowledge about trauma - important in my clinical practice.

I regret not having gotten to know Brooke, Blake, and their spouses John and Missy and their children Andrew and Eleanor and Katherine and Olivia, but hope that is an opportunity for another day?

In addition to his emotional support Jon was realistic and pragmatic: he soothed my teenage guilt about keeping my distance from the family while they paid for my college and medical school. In fact, I did not earn any money until I entered my internal medicine internship at the University of Florida in Gainesville. I try to see it as a trade-off: education and financial comfort rather than family warmth and poverty. All in all, I think my parents and my brother did a great deal for me - far more than I have for them. I regret that I never expressed my gratitude when I was growing up, although no acknowledgment of my appreciation would have changed the course of family history. I often think of these unpaid debts when I visit and order plantings for our parents' graves.

The most recent example of Jon's benevolence to me was to ensure that my family would have sufficient income to make it through our older years. I am thankful to him.

Acknowledgements

This book owes its life to those friends and family who urged me to turn my private musings – vignettes I had written trying to make sense of my life – into a memoir for others to read. At first, I wrote only for the family, but after a while I began to wonder whether there might be a wider audience for what I had to say. I sent a draft to my friend, Mitchel (Mike) Levitas who spent 40 years as an editor for *The New York Times* with that question. His response was a lunch where he told me that he and his wife, Gloria, an anthropologist, author and editor, would like to be my editors. And they have delivered, and for that I am truly grateful. Special thanks also go to Peter Petre, a highly regarded author and friend, whose thoughtful insights alerted me to ways of enhancing the reader's experience.

There have been others without whose help there would never have been a draft to send to Mike. Geraldine Powell, my brother's wife, read an early draft and focused me on the need to "show not tell." Alex Masters, their younger son, sent me more than 100 pictures he had culled from my mother's family albums which spurred my memories of my early life. Tamara Compton, Rosemary's brother's wife, did the genealogical research which allowed me to be more definitive about my forbearers. My cousin, Nancy Hanrahan, pointed out ways to organize the material to create a single story line from my two stories: the family secret and my life choices when the secret was no more. Bonnie Stretch, Rosemary's college roommate and one of our closest friends, applying her editorial skills on an early draft encouraged me to press on, that I was doing something important for my grandchildren and great-grandchildren.

However, without the love and support from my family, there would have been no book and no story to tell. Rosemary, who has been my partner through life, has read and commented constructively on every draft, always getting me to think more deeply about my experiences and my reaction to them. Kim has been supportive of my effort, contributing a gracious Afterword and wanting his children to learn from my experiences and particularly to understand the toxicity of secrets. Brooke and John and Blake and Missy encouraged me in my writing and brought me great joy.